W9-ANN-597

Best wishes,

Duane Noecker

Copyright applied for
Library of Congress Catalog Card No. 94-92166
ISBN 0-9641678-0-8

Cover: Grandpa talking with his oldest grandson, William Duane Hocker.
Gretchen, the dog, seems interested.

Printed by Kellogg Publishing Company Monmouth, Illinois

Contents

Dedication

In grateful appreciation, this work is dedicated to: My wife, Helen, who constructively criticized and edited it, and my former pastor, Rev. Howard Fawbush, who first suggested that I record these accounts of the sometimes incredulous activities of an unusual family.

Introduction

Those who have reached adulthood by the Twenties have become increasingly aware that we have lived our younger days in what amounts to another world. We grew up in the horse-and-buggy era; farm work was performed either manually or by horse-drawn implements. Railroads provided our only means of transportation over long distances on land. No electric power was available in rural areas, unless a farmer had his own generating system. Because there were no radio or television broadcasts, nor were sets available in our homes to receive such broadcasts, our rare treats consisted of going to town to "see the show" - perhaps a home talent production or a silent movie. Ours were simple days in those times.

Although nearly all of my grandchildren are fully grown already, other grandchildren and great-grandchildren sometimes ask, "Grandpa, what was it like when — ?" From our present facilities of almost instant communication all around the world, electronically controlled machinery by which a great amount of our tiresome work is done, and the ability to traverse long distances in a short time, we look back to "those days when —."

People of our age, watching television sets, have seen men walking on the moon, but we also like to look back at the times of our youth when life was much more simple. With the eagerness of a grandparent who wishes to draw an inquiring youngster into a closer fellowship, this Grandpa has attempted to bridge the gap of what seems to have been a few short years. He is calling for imagination of the young, as he hears them asking, "Tell me, Grandpa —," to note that while situations and surroundings may change, our problems remain basically the same. May these stories, drawn from incidents surrounding my ancestry, be helpful in connecting those events of a bygone age with our present manner of living.

In an attempt to faithfully portray those former days, I have relied entirely upon those stories which my parents and relatives have related to me; they were actual happenings. Claiming an author's right to use his own experiences, observations, and descriptive powers to picture these situations, I offer my grateful thanks to all who contributed to this view of former days that sometimes seem so long ago.

**The author –
Duane Noecker**

The author's parents -
Walter A. and
Gertrude Noecker
circa 1942

The author's grandparents –
Jairus and Mary Noecker

She is obviously pregnant, perhaps with Henry Augustus
who was born in 1877.

Chapter One
Grandpa

"Grandpa, tell me a story. Tell me about what it was like when you were a boy. What were your mamma and daddy like?" asked my grandson, Will. These were but a few of the other questions that followed.

"Wait a minute", I answered protestingly, "I can only tell you about one thing at a time!" I hesitated a bit, then began, "You see, things were quite different then. When I was a boy there was no radio or TV; very few people had cars, and airplanes were very, very scarce. Why, I remember, ---" and then my memory would lead me to incidents in my lifetime when I was a boy, and when - in a way - life was much simpler than it is today. It certainly was much slower.

Very similar questions came from my other grandsons and granddaughters, and I can remember asking the same from my Dad. Many were those precious times when I would be riding with him in the wagon while he went about doing his farm work. As we rode, he would describe in detail some of the fascinating incidents which occurred in his family when he was a boy. Being the twelfth of sixteen children in that family, Dad had witnessed and experienced a host of events - some of them almost unbelievable - which were woven into the fabric of that family's history.

From the memories of my childhood, as I presented them to a third generation, I frequently found myself comparing and contrasting my childhood and youth with Dad's. It was not long until an idea presented itself;

why shouldn't these be recorded in order that succeeding generations could enjoy them? The crutches by which I remember my favorite subject - history - are the colorful stories which constitute the warp and woof of the fabric.

I usually began as Dad did, "Well, one time when I was a little boy. —" and immediately I was engaged in bringing an image from the still-vivid past to the questioning time of the present. Perhaps grandparents who take time to tell such stories are the artists who paint, sometimes delicately - sometimes more vividly, the usually drab accounts of incidents and conditions which would otherwise pass into oblivion.

Aside from the joy that comes from being so close to youngsters, and of sharing vital experiences with them, is the hope that while doing this the story-teller may pass on the lessons, the dreams, and the ideals which are so important to people of all generations. Thousands of years ago, Solomon wrote: "Hear, my son, your father's instructions, and reject not your mother's teaching; for they are a fair garland for your head, and pendants for your neck" (Prov. 1: 8, 9, RSV).

Years ago I heard a story which I'd like to pass on. A young boy was being punished for disobeying his Dad's instruction not to use the sharp axe which his Dad kept in the woodshed. As his Dad bent the struggling youngster over his knee before the spanking, he scolded, "I told you not to use that sharp axe! You aren't big enough to handle it. You could cut off a hand or a foot with it! If I had done such a thing with my Dad's axe, he would have, —" and then Dad went on to describe his Dad's actions and authority.

"Yeah! I'll bet you had a heck of a Dad!" wailed the youngster.

"I sure did!" replied his Dad, "And a darned sight better one than yours!"

The Southern Michigan - Northern Indiana locale of Jairus Noeker's family.

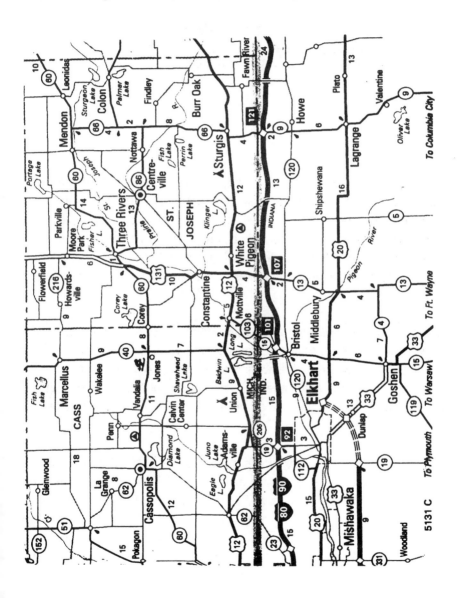

Chapter Two
Family Reunions

Having just returned from a family reunion, it is well to reflect on the observations we made as we associated with members of the family and greeted new ones (babies, in-laws, etc.). The reunion was a typical one; many relatives were from the vicinity, but a surprising number came from many miles away. There was the usual assortment of sizes and types which had assembled: fat ones, thin ones, weak ones, strong ones, young and old.

It is a sobering experience to realize that one's own generation is now the senior one. At one time we cousins were 52 in number; now only four remain, and only three of us were present. We looked back to the reunion of 1982 when our aunt, aged 99, attended. She had quipped that she looked forward to becoming a centenarian, because you rarely hear or read about anyone dying who is 100.

Aside from these personal experiences, some observations have come to my attention. Since the family genealogy and history is my responsibility, I persistently try to obtain additional information from any and all who attend. After the reunion I called on our oldest living cousin to obtain additional information (personal sidelights, anecdotes, etc,) which she might pass on regarding anyone in the family. Can you believe it? She couldn't stop talking about and showing the snapshots in her picture album, to give me the information I was trying so desperately to get.

This got me to thinking - are there those, in or out of my family tree, who just as earnestly have been seeking help, information, or assurance, and I have been too busy with my interests to notice or respond?

Our grandson, 15 years old then, made the 1982 trip with us. It was his first of this family's reunions. As we drove the 300 miles to return home we did a lot of reminiscing about the affair. Some pronounced family traits were quite evident. We had our favorites, and - because of certain actions, comments, etc. - there were those who had avoided becoming our favorites. Our grandson remarked, "Well, I didn't ask to become a member of this family, but here I am, anyway!' He made me wonder what members of the family had not listed me as being even near their list of favorites.

A surprise guest had arrived at the reunion; one cousin invited a man having the same family name as ours. In fact, his whole name coincided with the name of a member of our second generation (denoting my generation as now being the first). When he came we all tried to see if there could be any close connections between his family tree and ours. We all agreed that this would be a much more wonderful world if everyone looked for close connections with all others members of the human family, instead of emphasizing our differences. Mark 9: 38-41 records a teaching of Jesus which is pertinent.

We are all proud of our families, but how much more wonderful is the family of God. Most amazing of all is the fact that we are all adopted children. Galatians 4: 4, 5 states: "But when the time had fully come, God sent forth His Son, born of woman, born under the law, to redeem those who were under the law, so that we might receive adoption as sons" (RSV).

Chapter Three
Grandparents and Home Life

Some of the things we expect from grandparents besides the love which they always express in so many ways are: help during work peaks, counsel when asked for, and, yes, baby watching and teaching. There is another joy, however, which seemingly can come from no other source than our grandparents; it consists of listening to them as they reminisce about events which happened in their lives. I'll not begin with the usual: "I remember when, —" because I knew of my grandparents only through the stories which Dad and Mother told of them. (My last grandparent died when I was only four).

We all will concede that family life was a lot more rugged in those days; this was even more true for farm life. Perhaps this accounted for the fact that such manners of living drew families much closer together than they are today. Grandma Noecker could always be counted on to help in the field during harvest times. I've been told that when Grandpa cut oats or wheat with a grain cradle, it was Grandma who followed, picking up the loose piles of cut grain stalks, making a band out of a few stalks of grain, binding the piles into bundles (some people called them sheaves), and setting the bundles upright into shocks. Because there was such a large family, one or two of the older children would be under a nearby shade tree, tending the newest infant while Grandma worked in the field.

Dad related that after he was twelve years old, he worked as a farm hired man (hired-hand) at a neighbor's farm. Because Grandma had always considered that milking was a woman's work, Dad had not learned to milk a cow until he was in his late teens. It was then that as he had come home for a visit, he found that Grandma wasn't feeling well, so he offered to do the milking for her. After mild protestations she agreed to let Dad do this chore.

Picking up the milk pail, Dad headed for the barn. As Dad approached the cow, she started kicking; she fought Dad with every means available. It was as if she had said, "No man's going to milk me!" Dad had to resort to some strong methods of persuasion before that cow would allow him to take of her treasure. Even as he milked, she stomped, trying to stamp on his toes; she switched her tail at Dad as he sat there; she even threw her head toward Dad as if to try to butt him with her horns. As he brought the milk into the kitchen, Dad gave a blow-by-blow account of his struggle to obtain the milk which, because of the great effort taken in order to obtain it, was now recognized as being precious.

The anecdotes of Grandma's activities after supper are many. My Dad's most vivid memories of her at this time of day centered upon her sitting flatly in the middle of the parlor floor, sewing carpet rags together into very long strips which would later be woven into rugs. Grandpa would be seated nearby, for he usually read the news from the newspaper to her. All the while she might be using her foot to rock the cradle that held their youngest baby.

Grandma liked to cook, and family Sunday dinners were events to be remembered by everyone. Of course, as the family grew older, the older children of the family brought their spouses and their own children. It was not unusual on such occasions to have nearly 30 present. Grandma liked to bake bread and pies. I've been told that her specialties were baked beans and those large flat sugar cookies. (The family always expected cookies for breakfast).

How I wish I could have sampled some of her delicacies!

In the picture of Jainus and Mary is the parlor reed organ which must have accompanied the family during its trek westward from Pennsylvania by means of covered wagons. Several uncles and my Dad have related how the family used to gather around this instrument for a joyous songfest. It is my understanding that some of their favorites were: "Old Dog Tray", "Hail, Columbia!", "Old Black Joe", and "Old Folks at Home". Whenever they sang, "This is my own Native Land", they made a game of it. Coming to the chorus of the song, Grandpa would nod his head and sing, "Yes, yes, yes! This is my own native land." While Grandma sang, "No, no, no! 'Tis not my own native land." As they would finish, they often hugged each other and laughed. Grandma probably played the organ "by ear", and she was reputed to have had a very sweet voice. Because she spoke in the Pennsylvania Dutch dialect to her family and friends, she may not have sung much because she had difficulty with the English language. We can be assured that she and Grandpa must have sung many German songs together, though.

We often sing or hear songs about the Family of God. In Old Testament times the Israelites were called into holy convocations which must have been quite like great family gatherings. Especially during the Passover Feast, each family was gathered together to solemnly observe the time when God gave them deliverance from slavery.

Today, in New Testament times, we're called into convocation around our Lord's Table to worship and remember our Lord's suffering and death for the redemption from our sins. We, too, meet as one great family - the Family of God - and we reminisce about what our Lord has done for His Church and for ourselves as well. Paul wrote to the Church at Corinth that Jesus, during His initiation of this Feast of Love, said: "Do this in remembrance of Me" (I Cor. 15: 24c RSV).

I feel keenly disappointed every time circumstances cause me to miss out in attendance at any of these great family gatherings, honoring our Lord, don't you?

Chapter Four
A Face in the Window

What do we do when faced with a crisis? Still fastly indented in my memory is a story which appeared in a book by Canadian naturalist Ernest Thompson Seton, concerning a young mother cat with her first litter of kitttens. She had found refuge in a partly deserted cabin in the western mountains. One day, as she was caring for the kittens she was confronted by a rather large black bear who had entered the cabin, searching for food. In characteristic bear fashion, he was tearing open any cupboards or containers which he could find. Sniffing to determine the contents of each one, he then moved on to the next article to be examined and explored. Terrified, the young cat flew into a rage; she extended her fur as far out as was possible, then hissing and screaming as only cats can do, she jumped upon the bear's back, near his shoulders. Fastening her hind claws in his deep coarse fur, she clawed and scratched furiously at his back while she screamed cat-invectives at him.

Caught by surprise, the bear dropped to the floor, laid on his side, and vainly tried to dislodge the unrecognized beast on his back. Failing to do this, he became somewhat fearful of this unknown attacker. Without further attempts to repel his attacker, he ran to the nearest tree while the cat was still savagely tearing at his very tough furry skin. As the bear climbed the tree, the cat jumped to the ground, and with her tail still twitching nervously, she walked slowly back to the cabin. Once inside, she started nursing her kittens again.

Every generation has its particular crises; the changing times and situations determining each serious problem in detail. Obviously, each crisis may differ greatly from others, but the degree of intensity surrounding each one is surprisingly similar. Dad told me of an incident which occurred while he was a young boy, but first I'll have to set the background for a better understanding of his story.

During those years my Grandpa was out peddling in order to feed his large family. In wintertime he would be selling nutmeats and other delicacies to bakers and candymakers who were located as far away as Elkhart, Indiana, about 32 miles away from his home. This meant that he would be gone for one or two nights during each trip. His meager earnings dictated that the family would have to endure the strictest economy that could be devised. Undoubtedly, this was the reason why Grandpa felt it necessary to move to Williamsville, a tiny Michigan settlement which owed its origin to actions by the Underground Railroad before and during the Civil War. The Underground Railroad had a station nearby, and when the slaves were freed, those who had been enroute to Canada suddenly ceased being fugitives. Without any definite plans for the future, they set up several camps, two of which became Williamsville and Calvin Center. Life in those camps had been very primitive, and in Dad's time, about 30 years later, there had not been many changes. The postmaster's and Grandpa's families were the only whites in that little town of perhaps 500. Obviously, rent was cheap there.

The blacks were not only curious about how the whites lived; they also wanted to learn from the whites. They watched my Grandmother's actions very carefully, because they recognized her resourcefulness. One winter's night while Grandpa was away on a trip, Dad and his brothers were playing on the parlor floor near Grandmother who was also seated on the floor, sewing carpet rags. She looked up at the window, and the faces of her children were drawn to look there too. They saw the face of a black man with his hands on either side of his face, peering in at them. Grandma uttered a soft, "Ach!" (the German equivalent for, "Oh!"). Swiftly she rose to her feet. Grabbing a chair, she raised it above her head and headed for the window. The face vanished. Never did any thing like this happen again.

As Dad told me the story he admitted that he felt goose pimples all over his body, and that his scalp was rather tight. Dad said that he felt that the man was only curious as to how the Noeckers spent their evenings; he didn't seem to be malicious. When I asked what Grandma would have done if the black man had not run away, Dad answered that she would have crashed that chair right through the window. Apparently she did not know fear.

David sang a song of confidence (Psalm 27: 1-6). In verse 3 its climax cries out: "Though a host encamp against me, my heart shall not fear; though war rise against me, yet will I be confident" (RSV). We would do well to meet our emergencies with the courage of David who as a shepherd boy slew predatory animals, and even a towering giant.

Chapter Five
An Over-vivid Demonstration

Nearly a century ago my Grandfather Jairus owned a "thrashing rig" which consisted of a threshing machine - the forerunner of today's grain combine - and a steam engine to power it. The old engine was made by the Case Machinery Company. Because it had a small fire-box the operator of the engine had to constantly stoke it with wood to maintain the pressure and amount of steam which would be required to keep the machine operating. Even in those days it was recognized that to maintain safety whenever this machine was in operation, it was necessary for the operator of the engine to be very near it to stop it promptly. Because he was the oldest son, my Uncle Simon was selected for this responsibility. I am told that he was a very good operator.

The threshing machine was truly an antique by today's standards. One man was needed at the front of the "grain separator", as many called the machine, to cut the bands of the grain bundles, or sheaves, and then to feed the freed grain-laden stalks head first into the working parts. The separated grain - wheat, oats, barley, rye, or sometimes buckwheat - dropped to the bottom of the machine where it was carried by an auger to a set of half-bushel boxes which would be set on the ground beside the machine. Here a weighman "struck off" the boxes, running a straight-edge across each box to remove the excess grain on each box, making certain that the boxes were filled "level-full". His helper emptied the boxes into grain sacks for carrying the grain to the nearby granary while the weighman kept a tally of each filled box. A slatted canvas conveyor belt carried the threshed straw from the rear of the machine to the area where it would be stacked.

Such machines were considered to be complicated in those days; Grandpa was called the "separator man". His job was to keep the machine lubricated and adjusted for maximum efficiency and to ensure completeness of threshing. In addition to being alert for any warnings of a part in the machine which might show signs of advanced wear, he needed to maintain a constant vigil upon all workers to make certain that they took all the necessary precautions to work safely. Grandfather had always taken pride in his own safety record as well.

Lest I get ahead of my story, let me take you back to the winter preceding this particular harvest time. Grandfather and a number of his boys undertook to trim an overgrown hedge fence. The hedge was of osage orange, a yellow to orange colored wood which is very hard and tough. Its branches are always loaded with thorns which produce painful wounds that are slow to heal. Grandfather was piling some of the brush, getting ready to burn it, when one of the branches bounced backward, pricking his right index finger near the nail. Within a few days that finger became badly inflamed; obviously some part of a thorn had lodged there beneath the skin.

Refusing all offers of help, he wouldn't permit Grandmother or anyone else to attempt to prod and remove the foreign material. The family then urged him to go to the doctor for help, but he refused, saying, "It will work its way out". By harvest time, that finger, now fully infected, had swollen to twice its normal size, yet Grandfather refused treatment for the ailing member. The result was a very stiff finger that looked as if it was pointing at something or someone.

Threshing time came a bit early that year. Taking his "thrashing rig" out of the shed, Grandfather moved the rig to a neighbor's farm to begin the threshing season. He re-installed belts on the proper pulleys of the machine, then picking up his oil can having the longest spout, he prepared to lubricate all the bearings in the machine. He signalled Uncle Simon to run the rig at a slow speed while he squirted a generous amount of oil into the largest bearing.

Suddenly there was a loud groan of pain. His stiff forefinger had gotten caught between the belt and the pulley! Uncle Simon heard his dad's shout, so he immediately stopped the engine. Running to find out what was wrong, he learned that the machine's inertia had carried Grandfather's finger beneath the belt for a half revolution of its pulley.

By now Grandfather was jumping up and down, shaking his hand, loudly using every expletive he ever knew. Men gathered around to ascertain the cause of the uproar. An examination of the injured hand showed that the infected forefinger had burst open; pus and blood was dripping from the wound.

As soon as he could stand to work his injured hand to a reasonable extent, Grandfather signalled Uncle Simon to resume a slow speed for the machine. The owner of the farm where they were working had heard the disturbance; he came running up, demanding, "What happened?"

"O, this — finger!" replied Grandfather, "It's been stiff all year; it's infected. I couldn't bend it. See? I tried to oil this big bearing, like this —." To demonstrate his difficulty, he showed how difficult it was to reach that particular bearing. "See?" asked Grandfather again. In an instant the belt again caught the injured finger, this time taking it for two revolutions around the pulley. Grandfather is reported to have uttered every manner of vulgar and profane adjectives which had been heard of in that area for years.

My father, who had witnessed the accident, often expressed his amazement that the finger was not torn off Grandfather's hand that second time. The finale to the story is that, surprisingly, the finger healed soon afterward, and Grandfather seemed to be "none the worse for wear".

Moffatt's translation of Prov. 22: 3, 4 reads: "A cautious man sees danger and takes cover: a simpleton strolls on - and pays for it. On crooked courses men step into snares: a careful man avoids them".

Chapter Six
Grandfather, the Peddler

Grandfather Jairus was the oldest child of John and Priscilla Noecker, who had four other sons and four daughters. Jairus, being the oldest, was probably given a few more advantages than those which the others enjoyed. Family tradition has it that Grandfather Jairus was educated at the Freeburg (Freiburg, per the Pennsylvania Dutch spelling and pronunciation) Academy for the ministry. The building and its records were completely destroyed by fire many years ago, so legends must suffice for information about his schooling. Legends further indicate that Grandfather became disgruntled with the people with whom he worked. Their practice was not consistent with their pretenses, so he left the Church. The fact that he liked to talk and discuss ideas with people probably explains his natural gravitation to the art of selling. The time would have been approximately 1890.

Grandfather lived in a largely rural area, so his potential customers were farmers. In those times when money was not plentiful, he recognized the fact that, especially in wintertime, farmers bought little else than their necessities. Consequently, he undertook the role of a peddler during that season; this meant that he would have to direct his efforts towards the towns; that would be his marketing area. Instructing the boys of the family to gather all the nuts they could find each autumn, he made his preparations. The nuts were then carefully dried for processing.

On winter nights, immediately after supper, he and the boys would sit again around the kitchen table. Bringing out several pailfuls of these nuts, he set up his "shoemakers' repair last" which was normally used to repair the family's shoes; placing the nuts - one at a time on the last - he cracked the nuts carefully. As he passed the cracked nuts to the boys ' they would just as carefully pick out the nut kernels. They classified the nut-meats, because he sold the half-kernels to confectioners and candy-makers for decorating the tops of their products. The smaller fragments of kernels were sorted even further as to size, because they were used as ingredients for those candies and cookies. Obviously, the larger pieces brought the higher prices.

At regular intervals Grandfather packed his store of nut-meats in his spring wagon (called a "democrat wagon" by some) and set out on his round of customers. His farthest customer was a candy and cake-maker who operated his trade at Hotel Bucklen in Elkhart, Indiana. That hotel stood until it was demolished in the 1970's, and its distance from Grandfather's home was at least 30 miles. This obviously meant that he would have to stay overnight at some place near there.

He was reputed to be a very persuasive salesman, and his success of selling nut-meats caused him to branch out. He had the boys collect wild cranberries, water cress, and huckleberries when they were in season. These fresh delicacies he packaged and peddled along his route, and in a short time he had become a year-round huckster.

On rare occasions, during warm weather and on short rounds, he took my father along for company. During one such round, Grandfather stretched his sales day out too far, so he had to return home late at night. Dad was with him, and it was obvious to Dad that his father was lost. They came to a little village; all the lights were out, so it was apparent that everyone there was in bed. Grandfather stopped his team in the road in front of a house at the edge of town. "Hey, there!", he shouted, and he repeated, "Hey, there!"

After a number of calls, the man of the house raised his upstairs bedroom window and responded, "What do you want?"

"Where am I?" asked Grandfather.

The man answered, "You're out there in the road!"

Dad could tell by the tone of Grandfather's voice that he was quickly becoming exasperated, but Grandfather held his temper and replied, "I know that, but where does this road go to?"

"It doesn't go anywhere; it's been there for the last 50 years", said the man as he slammed his window shut.

"Then you can go to —!" exploded Grandfather; "Giddap!" he shouted at the team, and off they went. By about three A. M. they finally returned home, a very tired and sleepy pair of travellers.

At another time when my Dad was with him, Grandfather got lost again at night during their return home. Although Grandfather thought he recognized the town, he realized that it would be prudent to ask for information. Stopping in front of a house, he shouted out, "Anybody home?"

After a short time a man in the house opened a window and called out, "What do you want?"

"Is this Leonidas?" asked Grandfather. Leonidas was a small town about 25 miles east of Grandfather's home. He rarely traveled in that area to further his peddling activities.

"Just a minute," responded the man. He shut the window, and lighted his kerosene lamp. Grandfather and Dad waited an amount of time that seemed unbearable because of the cold weather, but finally the window opened again. "I dunno," he stated, "I looked and looked on the map, and I can't find it, so it must not be!"

"Giddap!" shouted Grandfather. For a long time they rode on in silence, then they began to theorize, searching for a meaning to that man's reply. Was he truly stupid? Was he just trying to make Grandfather and Dad the butt of a joke? What was the rationale for delaying his response to them? For years afterward Dad retold this story, but he never could reach an explanation for that man's behavior.

As we go on through life many questions arise and remain unanswered. The chapter, Proverbs 30, contains the sayings of Agur, son of Jakeh of Massa. The Moffatt translation of a portion of his writings, verses 18 and 19, reads: "Three things make me marvel, four things I cannot fathom: the way a vulture wings the air, the way a snake glides over stones, the way a ship sails o'er the sea, and the way of a man with a maid". As we continue our Bible reading for comfort, courage, and instruction, we often encounter passages which we do not understand. Some of these mysteries we shall never solve, but if we "keep on, keeping on", that's faith.

Chapter Seven
"I Like Them This Way"

In addition to his "thrashing rig", Grandfather owned a buzz saw which he powered with his steam engine. During the fall and winter, he did custom wood-cutting for the whole area. It was called it "buzzing-up woodpiles".

Those who have not been reared in the country need to understand that country folk in those times, as a matter of principle, always served meals to those who were doing work on their property. The buzz saw crew knew that they would be having noon meals wherever they were working. One of the places where Grandpa's crew worked was the Hartman farm where Uncle Simon had been working as a hired hand.

The Hartmans were frugal people and their life-styles were quite simple. Coupled with their manner of living was the fact that Mrs. Hartman was not a very good cook. The end result was that the crews who worked at that farm knew what to expect for their noon meal; she always served boiled potatoes and fried pork sausage, shoulder, or ham. One noon, as the hungry buzz saw crew sat down to dinner, she served them half-done potatoes. One man started to mash the potato on his plate, using his fork. The potato skidded off the plate, onto the floor. Another man tried to stick his fork into his potato; it merely rocked around on the plate, avoiding all efforts to prick it. Mrs. Hartman was embarrassed, so she said that if everyone would put his potato back in the pot as she passed it, she would cook the food a bit longer.

Grandpa, trying to be chivalrous, and undoubtedly because of his hunger, said, "That's all right, Mrs. Hartman, I like them this way". Saying no more, he used his knife to cut the potato into small cubes so he could chew the pieces without making an issue about the hard potatoes which had been served to them. A short time later Grandpa again ate at the Hartman's. He was surprised to see her remove two potatoes from the pot, set them aside, then continue cooking the rest for a few minutes before serving them. As you may have suspected, the undercooked potatoes were served to Grandpa, as a specialty for him. From that time onward, Mrs. Hartman continued to serve Grandpa thus, because he "liked them this way". Poor Grandpa never had the courage to tell her that he was just trying to ease her embarrassment.

We chuckle at his predicament. Possibly it seems all the funnier to us as we recall similar situations, perhaps some of them having happened in our lives. We recall that Jesus said, "Let what you say be simply 'Yes' or 'No'; anything more than this comes from evil" (Matt. 5: 37, RSV).

Admittedly, this teaching is difficult to follow, but then - who would profess that the Christian life has no challenges?

Chapter Eight
An Offer Refused

In lower Michigan it had been a long winter. Now that spring was beginning to make itself noticed, the ground was thawing, and the willow buds were swelling. All the farmers were looking eagerly toward their fields, making final plans for the crops they would soon be planting. The younger boys in Grandfather's household were playing in the barnlot, elated to feel the warm breezes which drifted up from the south. Like calves being released from their winter stalls in the barn, the boys felt like kicking up their heels, too.

Grandmother decided that she needed some fresh air, so, putting a scarf on her head, and throwing a shawl over her shoulders, she walked to the gate in front of the house. She called to Grandfather who was hitching his driving mare, Fran, to the road cart, "I'm going to go over to see Mrs. Lintz for an hour or so".

"Wait just a minute," Grandfather called back, "I'll take you there as soon as I finish hitching." Hurriedly he adjusted the last harness straps in place then drove up to the gate. Because of his peddling activities, Grandfather always kept good road horses. Fran was "a good traveler", as people of those times described road horses who could go long distances at a rather swift pace. Fran did have one bad habit, though; when she was hitched, as soon as someone touched the lines of her harness, she immediately started to go. Grandfather controlled this trait of Fran's by commanding, "Whoa!" as soon as he picked up the lines.

Unless he had a load to transport, Grandfather nearly always used a road cart when he travelled alone. This time he had hitched to the cart again, and as he stopped in front of the gate, he dropped the lines so that he could help Grandma climb into the cart. She had been standing on the step-stone which was used as a half-way point between the ground and the high buggies and carts which were their conveyances. Holding out his hand to assist Grandma, he pulled her into the cart, but, absent-mindedly, he picked up the lines with his other hand. Grandma was still standing up in the cart when Fran started to go forward at a brisk pace. Grandma fell backward out of the cart, landing with her shoulders on the ground and her feet high in the air.

Grandpa responded instinctively. "Whoa!" he yelled, sawing on the lines, as one does to control an unruly horse. Fran stopped and backed in an instant. The cart caught Grandma's heels and turned her backward in a complete somersault; she landed on her hands and knees in the chilly mud. "Giddap!" yelled Grandpa again, and Fran jumped into a fast trot. "Whoa!" he called again, looking back to see if Grandma was hurt in any way.

After pausing a brief moment to regain her senses Grandma got up, brushed some of the mud from her skirts, then started out along the road, walking as swiftly as she could, heading for the Lintz farm.

Meanwhile, Grandpa had turned Fran around toward the direction where Grandma was walking, and responding to his quick temper he struck Fran a couple of times with the end of one of the harness lines. Driving up alongside Grandma as she hurried on, he ordered, "Get in! I'll take you, and I'll handle this horse!"

"No! No! I won't!" Grandma sputtered as she came back at him with her Pennsylvania Dutch dialect, "I'll walk!"

Grandpa insisted, "Come on! Get in! I'll take you —."

"No, you won't!" was the reply, "I can walk faster than you can get me there!"

On they went, down the road; Grandma was still stomping angrily while walking as fast as she could. It was evident that only her pride and peace of mind had been injured. Close beside her proceeded Grandpa, driving a very nervous Fran, for he was still yelling "Whoa!", sawing her to a sudden stop. He then would hit Fran with the end of one of the lines, shouting "Giddap!", and off they would start. Thus they proceeded the entire three quarters of a mile to the Lintz home.

The boys had seen the entire string of events, and they watched in amazement, carefully controlling their facial expressions. When their arguing parents were well down the road, the boys doubled over with gales of laughter. Probably at that time, neither Grandpa nor Grandma could qualify as heeding the admonition of Prov. 14: 17: "A man of quick temper acts foolishly, but a man of discretion is patient."

Chapter Nine
Snake Stories

An aversion to snakes is common to most folks. Perhaps, because they usually lived near marshes in Michigan, perhaps because of certain isolated instances involving confrontations with snakes, there may have been some justification for this feeling which a majority of the Noecker family has shown. Elsewhere in this collection of family anecdotes there is an article dealing with snake-hunts which the boys of Grandfather's family conducted each spring as soon as the weather warmed enough to bring snakes out of hibernation.

Spearmint was a valuable crop to farmers who lived near marshes, and who were not opposed to committing themselves to laborious hand-work. As my Dad related his experiences to me, mint sprouts - or rootlets - were planted in marshy areas in early springtime. A single horse was fitted with pontoons on his feet. These pontoons were constructed of boards to form pads which were at least a foot in diameter; they were clamped to the horse's hooves. Equipped thusly, a horse soon learned to "spraddle out", as farmers called the wider stance which the horse had to take in order to avoid stumbling. A small sled was improvised for the horse to pull, and on this sled sat a man or boy who had a bucketful of mint rootlets. As the horse was driven along a line, or row, the driver planted these rootlets about a foot apart from each other. Probably all of us can appreciate the mint-planter's desire to be working in a snake-free area.

In August the mint had grown to where it could be harvested. The mint-fields, however, were still too soft to permit the use of a mowing machine to cut the lush green plants. This meant that farmers were obliged to mow the mint crop by hand, using scythes. A mowing-bee of farmers did this work, field by field, and Dad was usually one of these laborers.

When I was a young lad, Dad related a very unusual happening that occurred while he was mowing. Mort, the man who mowed the row ahead of him that day, was very scared of snakes, even the little ones. Suddenly Mort sagged to the ground, giving a muffled exclamation that ended with an "Ohhh!" As Dad hurried ahead to him, it was evident that Mort had fainted. Taking defensive action against anything which appeared near its nesting place, a blue racer, a constrictor type of snake which can glide quite rapidly, had wrapped itself around one of Mort's ankles, squeezing tightly to make use of its best defensive tactic. Having his own intense dislike of snakes, Dad grasped the attacking reptile just below its head, then, crushing its head with his heel, Dad struggled to unwrap it from mort's ankle. We can imagine Dad's own revulsion, as he fought the writhing body. Mort was soon revived, and mowing went on as usual.

Several years before this episode, Grandmother Noecker was hoeing in her rather large garden when she was struck by a copperhead, a very poisonous snake, one of the group of pit-wipers which includes rattlesnakes. Grandma knew at once that she was in grave danger, so, after killing the snake, she sat down in the corner of the garden. Calling one of her younger sons, probably Uncle 'Gust, she directed him to run to get the doctor who had his office in the nearby town. Apparently Dr. Slote, when he heard of the crisis, assumed that Grandma would be beyond all help by the time that he could get out to see her. He told the lad that Grandma should take a heavy drink of whiskey and remain as motionless as possible; he agreed to call there in the morning to see how she was progressing.

Returning as fast as his little legs could carry him, the boy passed the doctor's instructions on to Grandmother. She, in turn, directed him to bring out the whiskey bottle which she had hidden on the top shelf in the pantry. As he returned she told him to go to the field, calling for the men to come in to help. As he ran on this new errand, Grandma gulped down the entire contents of the bottle. (It had probably been more than half-full.) As the men arrived to carry her in to the house, they could see that Grandma was well on her way into a drunken stupor. She was a very strong woman, and in her state of inebriation she rolled and tossed, sang bits of German songs, shouted orders to children who had left home a decade earlier, then muttered incoherent phrases in the Pennsylvania Dutch dialect. One or more of the family remained at her bedside all night to try to give whatever assistance that was possible for them to give.

By the next morning Grandma was still alive, but she was experiencing a terrific hang-over which remained with her all that day. When Dr. Slote arrived at the home he, too, had difficulty in hiding his amazement in finding her still in the land of the living. For a week Grandma admitted that she was a bit weak, but afterwards she showed no ill effects from the ordeal.

Whenever I recall the family's account of this happening I recall God's curse upon the serpent that tempted Eve. It ended: "I will put enmity between you and the woman, and between your seed and her seed; he shall bruise your head, and you shall bruise his heel." (Genesis 3: 15, RSV).

Chapter Ten
Grandfather,
political poet

Grandfather Jairus had received what for that day was considered as an excellent education. Of course, the typical approved curriculum specialized in literature, mathematics, history, plus a certain amount of the classic languages, Latin or Greek. Probably due to some very good teachers, Grandfather fell in love with literature. Later, as the head of his family, he tried to see to it that all of his children were well grounded in literature also.

Always a decisive and outspoken man, Grandfather lost no time in making his opinions and convictions known. Being an ardent Democrat, he failed to see how others of a different political persuasion could possibly arrive at the political stands which they had taken. He faithfully attended all rallies which his party had staged in his community, and in his opinion William Jennings Bryan was the most suitable presidential candidate who had appeared during his lifetime. So dedicated was he in support of his hero that he wrote several parodies which could be sung using popular melodies of that day.

Based on the tune, "In the Year of Jubilo", a tune which was a popular pep-song for the Union Army during the Civil War, he wrote the lyrics to be combined into a song which was sung at nearly all the Democratic rallies which were held in lower Michigan that year. One stanza and the refrain ran like this:
"Say, voters, have you seen Mark Hanna,
McKinley and his crew

Have all crawled in a hole together,
And have pulled the whole in two.

Refrain:
"It's Bryan's day, Hey! Hey!
McKinley's done, Ho! Ho!
It sure must be that good times are comin',
In the year of Jubilo."

The gospel songs used by the Sunday Schools in those times were noticeably more militant than the ones we sing today. Harking back to Civil War days, "Hold the Fort" was a favorite song of nearly everyone. It was based on a message General Sherman sent to General Corse and his beleaguered garrison at the small fort at Allatoona, Georgia. As soon as he knew of General Corse's plight he sent smoke signals from his headquarters on Kennesaw Mountain. The message was, "Hold the Fort. I am coming."

Getting caught up in the fervor of the political campaign, Grandfather wrote a parody on this song also:
"Ho, my comrades, heed the issue
Coming from the sky;
Face the challenge of the spoilers,
Victory is nigh.

Refrain:
"So open the polls for the voters are coming
To cast their ballots in,
For if you vote for Bill McKinley,
It will be a sin!"

This song also became very popular that year; a number of male quartets added it to their repertoires as they sang for community gatherings. The applause which usually followed assured them that, disregarding political persuasions, the song had appealed to their listeners.

It is quite likely that as Grandfather wrote, he was reminded of Paul's encouragement to the Christians at Colossae: "Let the word of Christ dwell in you richly, teach and admonish one another in all wisdom, and sing psalms and hymns and spiritual songs with thankfulness in your hearts to God." (Col. 3: 16, RSV).

Chapter Eleven
Grandfather, The Orator

The three R's - Readin', 'Ritin', and 'Rithmetic were considered to be the essentials of formal education in the late 1800's. Because of farmers' intense needs for manual labor, their children were given only limited opportunities for academic learning. Many very successful farmers in those times had less than an eighth grade education, and those who had been graduated from high school were somewhat of a rarity. In addition, out in rural areas the terms of the grade, or grammar, schools were shortened so that the school terms lasted only through the winter, thus allowing the young people to help with the farm work which was so essential to a family's existence.

Grandfather Jairus was the oldest of the nine children in the family of my great grandfather, John Noecker. Possibly because he was the oldest, he was given greater opportunities or training than the rest of the family. There is evidence that Grandfather attended, and probably completed the course of study offered at the Freeburg Academy, Freeburg, Pennsylvania. Near the turn of the century a disastrous fire burned the building to the ground; all of its records were lost, so there is no known way to determine whether Grandfather was indeed a student there.

Because, wherever he lived, he was frequently called upon to deliver sermons, orations, or other speeches, it can be safely assumed that Grandfather had been a pastor, or minister. Being an ardent Democrat, he was often called upon to deliver speeches during political campaigns in nearby counties.

His speeches were well received because of their eloquence - a well-polished art for him. Eloquence enjoyed such a popularity in those days that elocution courses were offered in the curricula of most high schools. One day, as I glanced through the text book which my mother used, I found numerous illustrations in the margins of pages that depicted the various postures and gestures which should be used to deliver an effective speech. Hands extended toward the audience denoted that the speaker was entreating them to act or ratify his request, and the right hand raised and pointed upward indicated the statement or proposal of a truth or principle. When the speaker made a statement like, "Never shall —,"he extended his right hand, or both of them, forward with the palm facing the audience; this suggested that he was pushing himself away from the idea or situation. Students taking such courses were graded on how well they adhered to the standard prescribed for each type of statement or description. Can't you just picture a serious student standing before a mirror, executing the planned gestures and stances to be used while rehearsing a speech. A full-length mirror was needed, because the positioning of the feet was of vital importance also.

As far as can be determined, after his arrival in Michigan, Grandfather only preached for funerals or special occasions. He did seem to prefer giving political speeches, however, and according to those who were privileged to have heard him speak, he rose to the height of his powers when he urged his listeners to vote for William Jennings Bryan during the three times Bryan was a candidate for the presidency. During one campaign he made much of the Democratic Party's demand for the "free and unlimited coinage of silver"; Bryan was making his historic challenge, "You shall not crucify mankind upon a cross of gold!"

Grandfather demanded that his children, especially his sons, should also be orators to the best of each one's ability. Even though he had passed on many years before, whenever my uncles would be conversing during family gatherings, I noted that they invariably used eloquent terms to relate a happening, observation, or opinion. Perhaps Uncle Simon used this manner of speech more than the others; my memory vividly recalls his oratory as he described the first time he attempted to drive his new car.

Exemplifying his deep appreciation of hearing a well-rendered oral presentation, Grandfather often read aloud - always with good expression to give full meaning to the text. Poetry was his favorite form of literature, and he liked to sit back in his rocking chair with his eyes half-closed as he listened to one of his sons reading a favorite poem. That he was mentally transporting himself into the surroundings described by the author was evident. Those of the family who were called upon to do the reading usually did not share this pleasure, because as the reader would proceed, Grandfather would suddenly interrupt with a shouted, "No!", or "Hold on there! That's not the way! Here's how that should go." Then, taking the piece of literature, he would put all his feeling into re-reading the same passage. His younger children often jumped when his explosive outbursts interrupted their efforts.

Uncle John became an accomplished school teacher. He tried to instill in his students the art of eloquence, or at least reading with a definite meaning and feeling. As all teachers will attest that they have never been able to achieve all of their goals, Uncle John's achievements were also limited. During one period of his teaching at a rural grade school, he had a pupil, a girl named Emily, who absolutely insisted on reciting poetry in a sing-song fashion. When Emily was completing her eighth grade there, Uncle John scheduled the usual "last day of school" program, consisting entirely of recitations and dialogues, to demonstrate his students' proficiencies to their parents who were invited to the occasion. He had selected Rose Hartwick Thorpe's poem, "Curfew Shall Not Ring To-night" for Emily's recitation. Because this work is unfamiliar to many today, it should be stated that the last three lines of nearly every stanza in that poem remain the same.

When Emily arose and strode to the low platform at the front of the classroom, she took her stance, stiff as a cigar-store Indian, and began her typical style of oral delivery. In an effort to describe the emphases which she gave to certain words as she bored her listeners with her rhythmic monotony, I have underlined the words to which she gave greater emphasis:

"<u>And</u> her <u>face</u> was <u>death</u>-ly <u>white</u>
<u>As</u> she <u>said</u> with-<u>out</u> a <u>mur</u>-mur,
'<u>Cur</u>-few <u>shall</u> not <u>ring</u> to-<u>night</u>."

Grandfather had been invited to attend the event, and upon hearing Emily's presentation, he squirmed in his seat, often shaking his head. Finally, becoming so irritated by this sing-song delivery, Grandfather suddenly leaned over to Uncle John and hoarsely whispered, "Please excuse me while I go outside and relieve myself!"

In my imagination I can hear Grandfather using his oratorical powers to read the beginning passage of Psalm 19. Of course he would have been reading from the King James Version:

"The heavens declare the glory of God;
and the firmament showeth His handiwork.
Day unto day uttereth speech,
and night unto night showeth knowledge.
There is no speech nor language,
where their voice is not heard.
Their line is gone out through all the earth,
and their words to the end of the world.
In them hath He set a tabernacle for the sun,
which is as a bridegroom coming out of his chamber,
and rejoiceth as a strong man to run a race.
His going forth is from the end of the heaven,
and His circuit unto the ends of it:
and there is nothing hid from the heat thereof."

Chapter Twelve
Mrs. Lintz

No one in the family seems to know the exact year when Grandfather decided to move his family to a small farm on Millers Mill Road, near Constantine. Since he had rented the property, the St. Joseph county land records provide no data which will be of help. From other family records we can assume that the time was in the late 1890's.

Far better than the understanding of today's people, families in those days knew they needed to depend on each other. In less than two months the families nearby had met and accepted their new neighbors without any hesitancy. Probably because they lived nearby, George Lintz and his wife became good friends of the Noeckers, even though it was known that Mr. and Mrs. Lintz "didn't get along very well with each other". Dad often served as messenger-boy between the two households, but when he told me about them he never told me what Mrs. Lintz's given name was.

One early spring morning as Dad was bearing a message to the Lintz's, he could hear loud exclamations as he approached their home. To reach their back door he walked along the side of the house, when all of a sudden, George burst through the door with Mrs. Lintz close behind, brandishing a butcher knife. As he spun around to face her, George cursed, then shouted, "I hope that God will strike you off the face of the earth!" Turning back the other way, he saw the young courier.

Almost as if by magic George's demeanor changed. "Oh, hello, Walter. Come in and have breakfast with us", he greeted. Reluctantly, Dad entered the kitchen. Mrs. Lintz was calmly setting an extra plate on the table; there remained no evidence of the heated confrontation that had occurred a few moments before. Dad ate with them and returned home with their response to his message.

Possibly because of the enmity that existed between them, Mrs. Lintz seemed to be suspicious of others, and especially of men. Her suspicions must have become deeply rooted within her, because she was known to be the biggest gossip-bearer in the neighborhood. At that time Grandfather's work as a peddler required that he should be away from home most of the time. His route to Elkhart, Indiana necessitated his staying there overnight. That type of occupation was a catalyst to Mrs. Lintz's active mind. Her imagination suggested that Grandfather was involved in many infidelities, and that was probably the reason why the Noecker family was forced to get along on very meager finances. She didn't hesitate to communicate her suspicions to others.

When Grandfather heard of those tales he became very angry. He knew that Mrs. Lintz often came to visit with Grandmother, and although Grandmother had never confronted him about the gossip, he knew that Grandmother might naturally question his fidelity. Being a man of action, he promptly devised a plan to counteract these poorly-concealed acts of malice. He remained at home more frequently, each time he hid his road-cart behind the barn, so that if Mrs. Lintz came to visit Grandmother, Mrs. Lintz would assume that he was on the road somewhere. Not many days passed before he saw Mrs. Lintz on the road, approaching their home. Quickly using the outside cellar-door, he hid where he could at least faintly hear the ensuing conversation.

Mrs. Lintz knocked on the door, then entered. Soon after questioning about everyone's health, the conversation drifted off to discussing late news of the neighborhood. Those topics drifted into outright gossip. She soon questioned Grandmother about the frequency of Grandfather's nights away from home. Then came the suspicions: was he as loving as he formerly had been? Was it necessary for him to be away so much? He seemed to be spending more time in Constantine lately; was there a reason for this? The questions were followed by others like, "Have you heard that Mr. Blank was having an affair with Mrs. Doe?"

After quietly entering through the kitchen, Grandfather burst into the parlor. Without any greeting whatever, he confronted the gossiper. "Mrs. Lintz, I heard some of your lies about me!" he nearly shouted, "You're welcome in my house at any time, but I won't tolerate your coming here and poisoning my wife with your lies and gossip!" He concluded by stating with what she might expect if she continued to malign him and others.

Mrs. Lintz gulped and hastily left the house. Dad never told me whether the confrontation caused her to cease her gossiping, but he did say that she never brought any more wild accusations to Grandmother or her family.

The Bible has many warnings about gossip, but the basic one comes to mind: "Thou shalt not bear false witness against thy neighbor" Ex. 20: 16.

Chapter 13
Great-grandfather's Will

Nearly 30 years ago, while searching for genealogical information regarding my family, I looked through the records that were stored in the court house of Snyder County, Middleburg, Pennsylvania. Perhaps resembling a hound when he has just discovered a fresh scent, I looked through index after index, and finally I encountered my family name. Requesting the file clerk for the document that was listed in the index I came upon it. There I found the will of my great-grandfather, John Noecker. Surprised, almost astonished, I avidly read it again and again. Never before had I seen any evidence that would confirm the information about him which was passed on to me by my uncles and aunts. The dates referred to in it agreed with other family dates which I already had, so I knew that this must be the will of my great-grandfather; here was the proof I needed.

Clearly and beautifully written by hand, "The Last Will and Testament of John Noecker", was the heading of the document. The first sentence in the particulars of that will reads: "First, I do hereby debar my son, Jirus (sic) Noecker, from coming in and claiming any part as he hath already owed over four hundred dollars and never paid it back to me."

Finding this much information, I eagerly searched other files in various offices in the building. The additional information which I was able to obtain certified the information given to me by one of my aunts that my grandfather, Jairus, was the oldest of my great grandparents' nine children.

Also, I could deduce that in about 1876, Grandfather Jairus decided to leave Neitz's Valley and to "head out west". By that time he already had 10 children, eight of whom were still living, so we can understand his need to find better farm land. From my uncles I pieced together scanty bits of information which indicated that Grandfather had borrowed enough money from his father to buy perhaps eight horses and two or more covered wagons. Packing up, they headed for Indiana via the Cumberland Road. Today's U. S. Highway 40 roughly follows the route of that old highway which was sometimes called the National Turnpike.

Now, bits and pieces of family history began to make sense and to fit together. I feel sure that Grandfather's statement in his will was correct concerning Jairus' unpaid debt, because sixteen children were finally born into Grandfather's and Grandmother's family. It would have taken a miracle to feed, clothe and care for a family of that size, while paying off what was a sizeable debt in those days.

After a short stay near Connersville, Indiana the family moved on to Cass County, Michigan where the land was even poorer than that which they had left behind in Pennsylvania. My father often told many tales of the family's eking out the barest of existences there.

Why Grandfather Jairus made those decisions to move - especially why he left Indiana is a profound mystery to me. Information which has filtered down from others in the family indicate that grandfather was trained for the ministry. Why he persisted in trying to farm, when he had apparently been trained to be a clergyman, is another mystery for which I may never find the answer. It is reasonable to assume that Grandfather's farming methods were poor; if this is correct it is just another explanation for the family's poverty.

As of the date of this writing (1987) there is no information whether Grandfather ever seriously tried to pay back the debt he owed to his father, but I feel certain that he found the task to be quite impossible. Great-grandfather, however, expected full repayment of the loan; when he didn't get it he disinherited his son.

As I reflect on the meditations and experiences of this, or any other Holy Week and Easter, I marvel again at God's grace. How unlike the worldly ways of humankind He is! Great-grandfather was unforgiving; he expected "an eye for an eye and a tooth for a tooth". The psalmist said of God: "He does not deal with us according to our sins, nor requite us according to our iniquities," (Psalm 103: 10). If God were to expect restitution for our sins, our situation would be quite hopeless. Paul wrote: "For the wages of sin is death, but the free gift of God is eternal life in Jesus Christ our Lord," (Romans 6: 23). In one of his hymns Isaac Watts wrote:

"But drops of grief can ne'er repay the debt of love I owe;
Here, Lord, I give myself to Thee,- 'tis all that I can do."

Chapter Fourteen
Westward Ho!

During 1876 or 1877 my grandparents packed their meager possessions and their eight children and headed westward for a new start in life.
Behind them were the graves of two other boys who died in infancy. The
records in the courthouse of Snyder County, Middleburg, Pennsylvania show
that Jairus and Mary purchased two lots in the neighboring town of Freeburg
in May, 1873. In March 1874 they sold these lots, and late in that year
they entered into bankruptcy.

Upon reading the will of Great-grandfather, John Noecker, we find that
he disinherited his oldest heir, Jairus, because Jairus had borrowed four
hundred dollars from John and had never paid it back. My Uncle George,
the thirteenth child of Jairus and Mary, had often commented that when he
was a boy, he wondered why his father owned and kept so many horses on
such a small farm, less than eighty acres in all. As bits of family history
began to be accumulated and assembled, the reason for the horses became
evident. It is quite likely that four horses may have been hitched to each
wagon; by this arrangement the horses would not have had to pull so hard,
and extra miles could be added to each day's trek.

We can only come to the conclusion that Jairus had borrowed the money
to outfit his family for the migration westward. It is probable that he fitted
two, possibly three, wagons for the journey. During my childhood, my Dad
often described how Grandfather showed his boys how to use hot water to

soak narrow boards which had been newly sawn from green wood; after several days of soaking the boards were bent to fit between a number of stakes which were located to conform the boards into arches which would fit wagon boxes. These arches, when allowed to dry thoroughly, would be used to frame the canvas covers for the covered wagons which in those days were so essential for moving families over long distances.

Assuming that their travel began in early 1877, my Uncle Simon would have been sixteen years old; the next oldest boy, Harvey, would have been scarcely eleven. To conserve space and weight in the wagons, we may be reasonably sure that six of the eight children walked nearly all the way; the youngest of the six, Emma Catherine, would have nearly reached her seventh birthday. The remaining two, John (aged three) and Carl Edward (only two), must have ridden with Grandma. Without a doubt, Simon drove one of the teams; if there was a third wagon, Sarah and Susan probably shared the responsibility for driving that team. It was the custom of teamsters to walk along the left side of the teams they drove; each one using a jerk-line, a short strap tied to the bridle-bits of each horse and reaching over the back of the left horse which they called the "nigh" horse. The horse farthest away from the driver was called the "off horse". Many years later, when I was learning to drive horses, Dad taught me to hitch my team so that the shorter horse would be the nigh horse; that was just a tradition among teamsters. We can be assured that the teams they drove responded to the commands "Gee" (turn to the right), and "Haw" (turn leftward).

Pure logic tells us that the route used by Grandfather's family would have been along the Cumberland Road which later became known as the National Road. The Rand-McNally Touring Atlas, 1968, stated that this was our nation's first federal road; it extended from Cumberland, Maryland to Vandalia, the old capitol of Illinois. It was a toll-road, begun in 1811 and completed by 1852. Present-day U. S. Route 40 uses much of the right-of-way of the old road. Located fifteen miles apart from one another, some of the original toll gates still stand in Ohio, especially near Springfield.

The natural geography of Pennsylvania is such that the family may have passed along a valley between two ridges of the Allegheny Mountains, upward along Middle Creek then along Jacks Creek until it joined the Juniata River. Going upward along the Juniata, then up along Aughwick Creek they crossed a pass to where they could follow Licking Creek until it flowed into the Potomac River. Following the Potomac to the vicinity of Hagerstown they would have encountered more gently rolling terrain as they continued westward to Cumberland. The Cumberland Road led them northwest, back into Pennsylvania to the town of Washington, and then across the tip of West Virginia (Virginia at that time) to Wheeling. Encountering the towns of Zanesville, Columbus, and Springfield they crossed the state of Ohio, coming at last to Richmond, Indiana. Approximately twenty miles southwest of Richmond lay the smaller town of Connersville, and somewhere between the two, Grandfather settled his family. After a couple of years there, for some mysterious reason, Grandfather was on the move again. In this location there was good, rather level farm land; Uncle Simon recalled much later that Grandfather had raised good crops here.

Regardless, Grandfather repacked the wagons with the family possessions, and, picking up his family, they headed north-northwesterly to Cass County, Michigan. Here the soil was much poorer, but the family still depended on farming for a livelihood. We can be more sure of the dates of these journeys, because Uncle Henry August was born in Indiana, late in the year of 1877. Our scanty family records indicate that this move began early in 1879. In the Michigan section of the nation's 1880 census, my Dad is listed as a baby, one year old.

With all the modern conveniences that are now available to us, we marvel at the hardships which they must have had to endure. Assuming that the six hundred plus miles they travelled from Pennsylvania to Indiana was done in early springtime in order that Grandfather could get his crops planted for summer's harvest, we feel certain that they faced a number of storms enroute. I have often wondered how Grandmother cooked and how she fed her hungry family during the cold, windy, stormy days of that season. Also, where and how did each member of the family sleep? It is doubtful that they could have traversed more than an average of twenty miles per day. If that is true, the journey would have lasted more than thirty days. Reason, alone, reinforces what has been written about these travellers; there were probably no inexpensive places along the way where they could stop, bathe, and rest for a day before proceeding onward. The old Red Brick Tavern, located on the route, near London, Ohio, still stands. It has continued in business since before that time, but it would obviously have been too expensive for such a large family to make use of its facilities. We must conclude that the only water which the family used for drinking, cooking and sanitary purposes came from nearby streams or wells belonging to friendly farmers along the way.

Other questions arise. How did these folk maneuver their wagons up and down the steep slopes of the mountains? Dad told me that before travellers started down slopes which were very steep, it was a common practice to tie the rear wheels of each wagon so that they could not turn. In this way the teams literally pulled the wagons down these hillsides. Down severely steep grades, men often tied a rope to the rear axle of each wagon, then wrapping the free end of the rope around a sturdy tree they rappelled each wagon downward much like mountain climbers rappell themselves down mountainsides.

Going up such slopes, each wagon dragged fairly large triangular blocks behind each rear wheel. When it became necessary to rest the horses the wagons rocked back until the wheels rested against the blocks, thus holding the wagons in place until the horses could move their loads onward. Emergency measures were also taken; each wagon carried one or more stout poles which could be used as levers against wheels which threatened to bear their loads downward to serious accidents, if not outright destruction.

There was also the question of providing or transporting enough food for the people as well as the animals. I have heard that some families took a few cows with them so that they could start dairies when they became settled. We may well imagine that the animals were allowed to forage along the roadsides during the nights, but it does not take a lot of imagination to arrive at the conclusion that the people ate a lot of beans. Even that posed another problem: beans require a long time to cook; could Grandma have canned a lot of ham and beans, then opened the cans as needed? We do know that she always tried her best to keep her pantry and cellar loaded to capacity with all kinds of home-canned food. Uncle Simon was an excellent hunter, so he may have been able to provide some game for the table as they went along.

Those settlers proved to us one thing: they were survivors! Grandma relied on many home remedies to cure her brood when they were ailing. She depended heavily upon herbs and roots which she dried and kept ready to make poultices, teas, and the like for the cures she contrived. She never had to rely on a book for this information; it was all stored in her prodigious memory. People like her were our first paramedics, taught by experience.

We honor these early settlers; they were a restless kind of people. They eagerly kept looking for a better life for their families; they seemed to keep saying, "There has to be a better way!" As the writer of the Epistle to the Hebrews wrote his famous treatise on faith (Chapter 11) he concluded it thus and continued by encouraging his readers: "These are all heroes of faith, but they did not receive what was promised, since God had made provision for us to have something better, and they were not to reach perfection except with us. With so many witnesses in a great cloud on every side of us, we too, then, should throw off everything that hinders us, especially the sin that clings so easily, and keep running steadily in the race we have started. Let us not lose sight of Jesus, who leads us in our faith and brings it to perfection; for the sake of the joy which was still in the future, He endured the cross, disregarding the shamefulness of it, and from now on has taken His place at the right of God's throne" (Hebrews II: 39 - 12: 2 [Jerusalem Bible]).

Chapter Fifteen
An Overpositive Character

In trying to expand my genealogy records for my family, I keep encountering the name of Simon Kantz. My paternal grandmother was Mary Kantz, and I later learned that Simon was either my father's maternal grandfather, or he was Father's great uncle. As of the date of this writing I have not been able to positively determine my relationship to him. I do know that he and his family moved westward from Pennsylvania to Michigan, and I suppose his migration happened at about the same year that Grandfather Jairus also moved to the west. Simon and his wife, Sarah, came from an area where oil-shale and petroleum-bearing rock formations existed; in Michigan there was the sandy soil loaded with granite boulders of all sizes. From his boyhood Simon must have thought only of oil whenever he looked at rocks and stones.

The reason for his frequent visits with his relatives was perhaps because he was lonely - perhaps because he was now old and unable to do heavy farm work. At any rate, he often visited Grandfather Jairus, and sometimes he called on his grandson, (or his grand nephew) my oldest uncle, Simon Noecker. Characteristic of the old-world tradition, Uncle Simon Noecker always paid him every respect that was in his power to give. According to the stories about him, Simon Kantz sometimes took advantage of this deference.

Simon Noecker was a true craftsman; he had few tools, because he was poor. The tools which he did have were of very good quality, and he took extremely good care of them. Taking great pride in his ability to drive nails straight into hard wood - even oak - his prize tool was his carpenter's hammer. He never allowed his sons to use it, because he wanted to keep the face of the hammer as free of nicks and scars as possible.

During one of his visits Mr. Kantz walked out into a field where Uncle Simon was working. In Mr. Kantz's left hand was a broken granite rock; in his right hand was Uncle Simon's pet hammer! Before Uncle Simon could protest, Mr. Kantz stated very positively, in typical Pennsylvania Dutch dialect. "Simon! Dere ain't no oil in dese rocks!" Utterly shocked, Simon Noecker said very little, maintaining his respect for one of the older generation.

Wherever Simon Kantz went he could be counted on to make very positive statements about almost any subject which might come up. I suspect that he was a Christian Scientist, because during the winter that followed, when Grandfather Jairus, and most of his family was confined at home with the mumps, Simon Kantz appeared, knocking on the door. Grandfather met him at the threshold, saying respectfully, "You can't come in here now."

"Vy?" inquired Mr. Kantz.

"We've all got the mumps," answered Grandfather; "You'll catch them".

"I vouldn't accept of it!" snorted Mr. Kantz, starting to squeeze past Grandfather.

Grandfather still blocked the doorway; "You don't understand. This disease is contagious; you'll catch it. It makes you very sick!"

Still squeezing to gain entrance, he stoutly responded, "Nein. I vouldn't bodde(r) vid it!"

Grandfather permitted him to enter, and, of course Mr. Kantz shook hands all around, kissing some of the younger ones. Almost an hour passed before he left the house, untied his horse, got in the buggy, and headed for his home. A couple of weeks afterward, as all expected, he came down with a severe attack of mumps. From his neighbors came several detailed reports about his loud complaints and groanings.

According to my cousin, Harry Noecker, his father, (my Uncle Simon) often had blinding headaches. I suppose that they were of the migraine type. Anyway, one of those attacks struck Uncle Simon just as the threshing crew arrived and had begun to thresh his wheat. Because of vertigo, he could barely stand, so he excused himself and went into the house to lie down and recover his equilibrium. The crew kept on threshing.

Within the hour, Simon Kantz arrived at the farm to see what was going on there. Going out to where the threshing was taking place, and finding no trace of his namesake, he walked to the house. There he found Uncle Simon lying on the sofa; the shades were drawn, and Uncle had a damp cloth on his forehead.

"Simon! Vy ain't you oudt dere tressing?" demanded the visitor.

"I've got a sick headache, and I can't stand on my feet," replied Uncle. "I've told them what to do, and what was wrong with me. I got so dizzy I just had to go to the house. I can hardly sit up now", replied Uncle.

Although Simon Kantz knew his namesake was a very hard working man, his stubborn pride took over. He exploded: "Simon! You say you ain't sick, undt py dam', you ain't sick!" Without saying anything more, he stalked out of the house, got in his buggy, and drove off toward his home. I can imagine him muttering to himself as he went, "I vouldn't accept of it!"

Not long ago I noted a verse among the proverbs of Solomon; Prov. 25: 14 and 27. Per KJV, it reads: "Whoso boasteth himself of a false gift is like clouds and wind without rain. For men to search their own glory is not glory". Perhaps I have been too hard on Simon Kantz, but according to family stories which have been handed down to my generation, his way was always right and he was not a bit hesitant to make that known to others.

Chapter Sixteen
Rover

Although I never saw him, I feel that from the tales my Dad used to tell, I almost knew Rover quite well. You see - Rover was a dog; he belonged to Grandfather Jairus and the family. The reason I describe his ownership in this manner is that I can not recall my Dad's mention, even once, of Grandmother ever having had anything to do with old "Rove". Primarily, Grandmother was entirely too busy with her colossal task of mothering such a large family that she had little time for dogs - or cats, for that matter. It is also probable that she felt that dogs were for boys, for most boys have a natural affinity for canines, and it seems that dogs naturally turn to boys for companionship and understanding.

From Dad's many stories about "old Rove", I pictured Rover as showing a descent from a bulldog ancestor, and I suppose that the rest of his ancestry was just "dog". The mental picture that I have of him is that he would be of medium size, about as tall as an English bull-dog. I understand that his color was what Dad described as "brindle" - a sort of medium brown containing spots and streaks of darker brown. His hair probably was of medium length, and likely, his legs were even shorter than average for a dog of that size.

Probably there was a total of six boys living at home during Rover's lifetime, and being typical boys, they all claimed him. That alone would provide a main source of arguments among the boys. According to accounts which my uncles told about him, he was a natural watchdog; other than that, however, Rover had few other good attributes. That was probably due to the fact that he must have been a very confused dog. From the time when he joined the family as a pup, the boys would gather around him, each one whistling and calling to him at the same time, each vying for his attention. Rover seldom knew which boy to obey.

We would be very naive to suppose that those boys did not tease Rover somewhat; isn't it quite natural for boys to do this? As Rover grew older, he protested being the butt of boyish pranks by suddenly biting one or more of them. When "old Rove" had reached the end of his patience, he would suddenly start to chase them with teeth bared. At such times each lad sought safety by climbing the nearest tree. As may be expected, there were times when old "Rove" kept them in the trees longer than they desired.

Dad told of another time when his next older brother, my Uncle 'Gust (Henry August) was petting Rover, growling at him in mock ferocity. "Old Rove" didn't quite know what to make of such a portrayal, so he resorted to a dog's instinct: "When in doubt, attack!" With a loud growl "old Rove" suddenly rushed at Uncle 'Gust with open jaws. Instantly, 'Gust could see that there was no time to run to a tree for safety, so he quickly clenched his fist and shoved .,it down the dog's throat. Surprised, Rover could scarcely get his breath, let alone close his jaws. Backing away, and gasping for breath, poor "old Rove" retreated to his dog-house, gagging as he went.

One of the still-existing stories about Rover came from the time when the family was living in Williamsville, Michigan during the late 1880's. The town was almost totally populated by African Americans who had been slaves, or were children of slaves, and who had escaped from the South via the Underground Railroad before or during the War Between the States. When the Emancipation Proclamation grew into the Thirteenth Amendment to the Constitution, all slaves were freed; there was no longer any need for these people who were escaping from slavery to travel further into Canada. Resorting to natural instincts, they just set up very simple camps in Michigan. One of these camps, located on Shavehead Lake in Cass County, became Williamsville. Because their older generation had not been privileged to own more than the clothes on their backs, they had only the barest of necessities. Consequently, these people had little or no regard for the ownership of personal property; if they saw something that they wanted, and if the opportunity presented itself, they took that "something."

My father related the incident which happened during the family's residence there. Grandfather had just butchered a couple of hogs to provide meat for his big family. After he cured the meat by rubbing it with a salt, salt-petre and pepper mixture he stored it, hanging it downstairs in the cellar which had only an outside slanting "cellar door" for an entrance. One or two evenings after the meat was hung up, Grandmother said to Grandfather, "I hear something downstairs!" Grandfather kept on with his reading, saying she was imagining something. She insisted that she heard something, so Grandfather took Rover by the collar, opened the cellar door and said, "Sic 'em!"

With a big growl Rover rushed into the cellar, and a moment later he rushed back out with the rapid barking sound of a dog who had just about closed in on his prey. A minute or two afterward he came back, and Grandfather brought him back into the house. The next morning they found a patch of cloth about eight inches square hanging on the back fence. A day or so later they noted that a man living nearby wore a big patch of that approximate size on the seat of his pants. No more meat was missing after that incident.

Sometimes we are somewhat like Rover when he was a puppy. We hear many calls to follow false gods; there are calls to pleasure, wealth, power, or fame. Cults and false religions also call, and if we are not prayerfully watchful, we, like a confused puppy, may respond to the tempting call. Jesus said to His disciples: "The days are coming when you will desire to see one of the days of the Son of man, and you will not see it. And they will say to you, 'Lo, there!' or 'Lo, here!' Do not go, do not follow them," (Luke 17: 22, 23 RSV). We may recall a stanza of a hymn written by John E. Bode (1816-1874):

"O let me feel Thou near me! The world is ever near;
I see the sights that dazzle, the tempting sounds I hear;
My foes are ever near me, around me and within;
But, Jesus, draw Thou nearer, and shield my soul from sin."

Chapter Seventeen
Push ahead, or Wait

Sarah Heinselman Kantz must have been an unusual woman; she may have been the mother of my grandmother, Mary Kantz Noecker. (In this article I'll refer to her as Great grandmother.) She and her husband, Simon, a plodding farmer, were both from Pennsylvania Dutch families. The dialect used by these people holds a whimsical fascination for me, so I will try to phonetically portray their conversation as it is recalled.

For a time Sarah taught in the public grade school near her home. A woman once asked her concerning her methods and successes, and Great-grandmother replied, "I chust puts de echsample (example) on de poard (blackboard), undt vitch vun dot kin do it, vitch vun push ahead". (We sincerely hope that her student body was entirely made up of Pennsylvania Dutch children, and we take comfort in knowing that teaching standards have been improved greatly since then).

From all recollections of her, she must have been a woman to truly "push ahead". Indeed, it was a requirement for all farmers' wives in those times to push ahead. Great grandmother could not be easily distracted from achieving the goals which she had set up for herself. Some women, while visiting at her home noted that her pantry cupboards seemed never to contain any remains from a previous meal; at times they asked her what she did with her left-overs. "I chust keep puttin' it pack (back) on de table, till he duss (does) eat it", she replied.

Wood was the universal fuel for heating and cooking in those days. It was Great-grandfather Simon's, responsibility to maintain an adequate supply of firewood, and she laid down strict requirements for the wood she would be using. One day when he came in from work she announced, "Simon, I need holtz (wood)".

Simon was thinking about some other things when he answered "Ya, Sarah". He sat down to eat, and nothing more was said about wood at that time. During later meals his wife's repeated requests for wood seemed to fall on deaf ears; he calmly answered each reminder with his, "Ya, ya!" and continued with whatever had captured his attention.

Not long afterward, he came in from the field at noon, dog-tired and bear-hungry. With a farmer's typical appetite, he sat down at the table; he noticed that his plate contained a big slice of ham - uncooked. Beside it were two medium sized potatoes, also uncooked. "Vy Sarah!" he exclaimed, "Vas nennte dis? (What does this mean?)"

Pointing to her empty wood-box she emphatically, yet calmly replied, "Holtz!" (wood).

Without saying anything more, her husband lowered his head, got up and plodded out to the pile of uncut logs laying near what had been the woodpile. An adequate supply of wood appeared beside the cookstove in a very short time. We may presume that Great-grandfather had to wait a quite some time later for that meal.

Perhaps all of us are tempted at some time or other to procrastinate; with others, procrastination is a persistent habit. Proverb 27: 1 (R S V) states: "Do not boast about tomorrow, for you do not know what a day may bring forth". James 4: 13-17 is the New Testament confirmation of this truth.

The adamant reluctance of unbelievers to accept the invitation of Christ to follow Him and to make Him Lord of their lives is a dismaying thing to all Christians. Worse, there are many who know that they should make that significant change in their lives, yet are habitual procrastinators. When Paul was in prison in Caesarea he had the opportunity to witness for his Lord before Felix, governor of the province of Judea. Acts 24: 24, 25 (RSV) records: "After some days Felix came with his wife Drusilla, who was a Jewess; and he sent for Paul and heard him speak upon faith in Christ Jesus. And as he argued about justice and self-control and future judgement, Felix was alarmed and said, 'Go away for the present; when I have an opportunity I will summon you'". With regret we note that there is no record of his later acceptance of Christ.

Chapter Eighteen
The Enforcer

When I was a young boy I often crawled up on my Dad's lap, eagerly asking him what it was like when he was a boy; I loved to hear those stories of his youth. Now that I have become a grandpa, one of my chief pleasures is that of recalling my boyhood days, and relating these incidents to my grandchildren. When it comes to the vast number of available stories and the adventure and excitement contained in them, Dad's stories excel mine by far. It has frequently been mentioned before that Dad had eleven brothers and four sisters, and it goes without saying that a family of that size provides an automatic guarantee for plenty of stories - all of the human interest type.

As you can well imagine, a family of that size was often confronted with disciplinary problems. As I sat on my Dad's lap, I often heard of his father's "enforcer". It was a piece of razor strop about a foot long, and it was nailed securely to a wooden handle. When it was used for a spanking, it not only hurt, but it made a lot of noise as well.

Many of Dad's stories were about the fights that broke out among the boys. Often the fights or quarrels occurred while they were playing on the floor after suppertime. Their father, if he were home that evening, would be seated in his favorite rocking chair, reading. All he needed to do to stop the altercation was to look above his eyeglasses at them and say, "Boys!" If the disturbance didn't stop immediately, the enforcer would be put to use. There were times when as many as six boys would become involved in a commotion. When they were confronted by Grandpa one of them would almost invariably point at another and burst out: "He started it!"

This never had much effect on Grandpa. He could be counted on to respond, "Never mind! I'll get the right one!" According to my Dad's stories, Grandpa always picked up his enforcer and did as he promised.

Dad frequently recalled a particular time when he felt the influence of the enforcer. According to his story, he and Uncle George were teen-agers. A neighbor, living a couple of miles away, had invited all the folks nearby to a square dance to be held at his home. Telling Grandfather Jairus about it, they asked for permission to attend. Somewhat gruffly he responded, "It's all right for you to go, but just remember - we've got to get up early tomorrow; there'll be a lot of work to do in the morning!"

Thanking their father, they gleefully made plans for the great evening which was only a few hours away. As soon as the evening meal was finished, the two teen-agers put on their clean shirts and overalls, and, saying, "Goodbye," to the family, they hastened to the neighbors' house. Time passed so swiftly there; before they realized it, it was past midnight.

Hurrying home, they chuckled at some of the events which had occurred that evening. As they scrambled into bed they immediately fell asleep. It seemed to them that only a moment had passed before they heard Grandfather call out, "Boys! Get up! It's half-past four!"

They had no chores to do, and knowing that Grandfather usually took about a half hour to do his, Uncle George told Dad, "We've got enough time to get a few more winks; we'll hear Mother when she puts the frying-pan on the stove, then we'll jump into our clothes and be at the table, ready, when Father comes in".

The next thing they heard was Grandfather asking, "Are the boys up?" Dad said he instinctively knew that it was already too late to begin dressing. In a moment Grandfather was there, enforcer in hand. Accompanied by a short lecture there was the sound like, "Whap! Whap!" as the enforcer was put to use. Dad concluded, saying that after many years had elapsed, he could still vividly remember that painful morning.

As an only child, growing up on the farm, I felt that I was rather shut off from the rest of the world. It therefore followed that what I did or thought would not affect others much. Those independent ideas of mine went on for a while until I began to realize that my selfish attitudes and reactions with others were causing them to be aloof and sometimes actually hostile toward me. John Donne wrote: "No man is an island, entire of itself; every man is a piece of the Continent, a part of the main".

Looking back to the days of my military training, I remember incidents when thefts occurred in a company of servicemen. If the missing article did not reappear within a specified time the whole company was disciplined; all suffered the same punishment. There are many to-day who would protest, as I secretly did then, that this sort of treatment is unfair. Later, during a particular chapel service, the chaplain based his sermon on a statement which Paul made as he wrote to the Church at Rome: "None of us lives to himself, and none of us dies to himself" (Romans 14: 7, RSV). We recognize that Paul was writing about a different idea, but as I listened to that sermon I had to reason that this truth applied to my situation as well.

Reflecting upon the incidents which happened in Grandpa's family, plus my own personal experiences, this truth becomes clearly evident: we all suffer together for the misdeeds of one or of many. Paul wrote to the Corinthians: "If one member suffers, all suffer together; if one member is honored, all rejoice together" (I Cor. 12: 26, RSV). Nearly everyone loves to sing John Fawcett's hymn, "Blest be the Tie that Binds". He was a pastor in Wainsgate, Yorkshire, and had accepted a call to a church in London. With all his family's personal belongings packed and loaded for moving, he said, "Good-bye", to his congregation. Their grief at his leaving caused him to unload and remain with them. Shortly afterward he wrote the poem that became this hymn. Stanzas two and three read:
"Before our Father's throne
We pour our ardent pray'rs;

Our fears, our hopes, our aims are one,
Our comforts and our cares.

"We share our mutual woes,
our mutual burdens bear;
And often for each other flows
The sympathizing tear."

Chapter Nineteen
Diamond Lake

Less than a mile east of the town of Cassopolis, county seat of Cass County in southern Michigan, lies the sparkling, beautiful Diamond Lake. It is somewhat larger than most lakes in that area, being approximately two miles long and as many miles wide. Being somewhat diamond-shaped, it may have been named because of its shape. Every time I see it, however, its wave-rippled waters sparkle in the sunshine like a cluster of diamonds, and I suspect that the early settlers when they, too, noted this spectacular beauty, may have exclaimed, "Why! This lake has the sparkle of diamonds!"

A lot of Noecker history has been centered around this lake. Although Grandfather's family often lived as far as ten miles away from this body of water, it so impressed them that they used it for a common expression. Grandfather and his sons often remarked, "That's as far away as Diamond Lake!"

Many years ago, a couple of my cousins left the farm where they had been raised and had found jobs in a cereal factory located in Battle Creek, quite a distance away from their home. After having spent nearly all of their daylight hours at hard labor on the farm, they now rejoiced in the fact that they now had time to take up golfing for recreation. During one of their visits home, their family went to "see Grandpa and Grandma". After the traditional Sunday dinner the cousins got out their golf clubs and said that they would show their dad and others how to play the game.

Of course there was the usual Noecker banter; the young men - thinking that their dad, my Uncle Clyde Latshaw, would miss the ball the first one or two swings, and then would probably slice the ball, causing it to get lost in the nearby woods - made a bet with him. Pointing to a tree located about 250 yards from them, they bet him a dollar that he couldn't drive the ball as far away as the tree. More than that, they allowed him three drives to go that distance. I think it was Irwin, the older one, who set a golf ball on a tee, then, handing a driver to his father, he explained, "Here! you hold your club this way —," and he demonstrated how the professionals held their clubs as an aid to insure a good drive.

Uncle Clyde, who was a natural athlete, shook his son off, saying, "Let me alone! I know how to hit a ball with a stick!" So saying, he walked up to the ball and hit it squarely. My dad, who had witnessed all the banterings, estimated that the ball travelled well over 300 yards distance, well beyond the tree which had been the goal. "There! Give me my money, and go get that darned ball! If I hit it two more times, you'd have to go over to Diamond Lake to find it!" exploded the victor. Then, turning to the rest of the men who had gathered to watch, he continued, "Walt and me used to hit them darned things when they threw them right at us!" as he referred to the times when he and my dad had played baseball together. He then walked away as everyone laughed.

Perhaps the family's frequent referral to this lake was due to an offer which was made to Grandfather a number of years before then. This lake offered an added attraction to people in the area; it had an island which was located nearly in its center. Being round and nearly a quarter of a mile in diameter, it was a favorite picnic spot. Families borrowed or rented boats and rowed over to the island, picnicked there, then rowed back to where they had left their carriages. A man, whose name I never learned, owned the island; he also owned several boats which he kept in readiness for renting to picnickers and those who just wanted to go for a boat ride.

One fall, after picnicking was over for another year, the owner of the island offered to trade it to Grandfather for his team of horses. Possibly the man had come to the reality that he should be taking life a bit easier; I think he had been running a concession stand in conjunction with his boat rental business. Since Grandfather always kept good horses, it would have been considered a fair trade by most people of that day. Coming from the center of the Pennsylvania Dutch country, Grandfather loved horses, especially the better ones. After a short period of thought, Grandfather refused the offer.

Why would he come to this decision? His reasoning probably went something like this: "I have a large family to support. I should keep on being a farmer; we can raise most of our food there. Income from a farm has got to be greater than what he is making at the lake. He is offering no other land than that island; I can't farm it, and, besides, there is no income from that island from September to May. How would I feed my family? And if I did make the trade, what would we do for transportation? I have no other horses than this team. Even if the island would make a good investment, I can't afford it; I have to be concerned about the present".

Today, this island contains at least a hundred rather substantial residences; it is inhabited during the summer by people who are financially well situated. The dwellings are privately owned and acknowledged to be expensive. Some of my relatives have commented disparagingly regarding Grandfather's apparent lack of foresight in refusing to make the trade. Personally, I think Grandfather did what he had to do. He had to be a realist; he did not even dare to think of "pie in the sky", as we often refer to optimistic day-dreams.

During His Perean ministry Jesus taught about making plans and then considering the costs of such endeavors. The NIV translates Luke 14: 28-30 in this manner: "Suppose one of you wants to build a tower. Will be not first sit down and estimate the cost to see if he has enough money to complete it? For if he lays the foundation and is not able to finish it, everyone who sees it will ridicule him saying,'This fellow began to build and was not able to finish—' ".

Chapter Twenty
Uncle Fred

Being the youngest in a family of 16 children, Fred H. Noecker had to contend with his status of being the "baby of the family". Most of us are, aware that this chronologically late entry into a family can have both advantages and disadvantages. His brothers and sisters, as you can well imagine, often complained that this junior one was "being babied too much". We can only surmise as to whether or not this was true.

For some reason Uncle Fred was afraid of the dark. From someone else in the family came this tale. Before going to bed, as he prepared to go outside to take care of the needs of nature, he opened the door. Quickly he jumped back inside and slammed the door. "What's the matter?" several asked.

"I just looked outside when somebody said, 'Oh, no!'" was his reply.

A brother then opened the door, and he heard their rooster crowing. The report that Fred had heard a rooster caused the whole family to laugh heartily.

Another incident, as related by my father, occurred when Uncle Fred was in his early grade school years. Everyone in that large family had his or her work to do, and by the time Fred was about six years old he was saddled with the responsibility of keeping an adequate supply of wood in the kitchen wood-box at all times. To Fred, that large wooden box which was located near the cook-stove seemed to be nearly empty most of the time. Wood was Grandma's only fuel, and the tremendous amount of cooking that was needed for such a large family demanded frequent wood-box re-fills.

With a six-year-old's typical preoccupation with the many curious and mysterious things around him we can understand the lack of attention which youngsters give toward their responsibilities. Apparently Fred fitted in well with the frailties of that age group. Grandma frequently had to remind her young son of the lowering supply of fuel in the box. "Fred, bring me some more wood; the wood-box is empty", she asked one evening as she made preliminary preparations for food which she had planned to serve the   next day. Understandably, he delayed the performance of his assigned chore, because darkness had already settled over the land. Although he had very few toys, he kept playing with them, perhaps thinking that if he kept delaying the chore long enough, someone else would do the job.

"Fred," Grandma complained again after a short time, "I need wood!"

There was no answer. Everyone in the family knew that Grandpa didn't like to be disturbed when he was reading the weekly newspaper, and this evening he was enjoying this pleasure. He had scarcely noticed Fred's lack of response to his mother's statement, but there was something in the quality of her voice that demanded his attention. He slowly looked up over his newspaper, and with a commanding voice said, "Fred!"

Grandfather was like the typical stern schoolmaster of his day; he was a rigid disciplinarian. Whenever any member of the family heard an order like that, he or she knew that instant obedience was required. Quickly jumping up from the floor, Uncle Fred hastily put on his coat and cap and lighted their kerosene lantern. He knew that he could delay no longer. He sighed heavily as he headed outdoors, muttering audibly, "Some day they're going to miss me around here - when I'm gone!"

Perhaps, at one time or another, we may feel as Uncle Fred did, but during such periods we need to remember that in God's sight we are all very important. If this were not true, John 3: 16 could not be in the Bible. As a precaution against our feeling too important, however, it was Jesus who said, "He who is greatest among you shall be your servant; whoever exalts himself will be humbled, and whoever humbles himself will be exalted" (Matthew 23: 11, 12 RSV).

Chapter Twenty-One
Uncle Bob

One of the Noecker uncles whom I never knew was named Robert Lee Noecker. He died of tuberculosis at age 15, which is 24 years before I was born. Regardless of that, those who were near to him spoke of him in such glowing terms that I feel as if I knew him rather well. Their stories must have been basically true, because our family records indicate that when he became seriously ill, he spent the last six to nine months of his life with the family doctor. The newspaper account of Uncle Bob's death states that Dr. E. P. Partlow who lived in the nearby town of Constantine had taken Uncle Bob to live with his family.

Uncle Bob loved fun. Everyone agreed that he was a terrible tease, but his innocent appearance and disarming smile usually removed his victims' urge to become irritated, even angry with him. His almost obsessive desire to "get someone's goat", as people of that day expressed exasperation, could have gotten him into trouble many times. Each time, that uncanny knack of Bob's in carrying out his various acts of teasing with a childlike air of innocence usually resulted in hilarious amusement for all who witnessed his pranks. Because they recognized that his health was frail, it is possible that all of his family made allowances for his puckish behavior.

Grandfather Jairus was a typical German head of the family. He worked hard, but when he came home for the evening he expected his children to get things for him and to do other little chores. Using an idiom of today, we would say that Grandfather had a rather "short fuse". One might easily deduce that Grandfather's large family probably contributed to this characteristic.

A favorite anecdote of the family relates that Grandfather was sitting in the parlor, pursuing his favorite pastime - reading. Looking up over his glasses, he said, "Bob, go upstairs and get me a pair of socks". Uncle Bob dutifully got up from the floor where he was playing, climbed the stairs, and soon returned with two socks folded together. He handed them to his father, who took them, looked at them, and exclaimed, "I wanted a pair of socks".

Bob, who was standing nearby, answered, "I brought you a pair".

"But they're not alike"', explained Grandfather, in a manner which he used to explain things to children, "One's brown; the other one is blue".

"They must be alike; they were together, and they're the same size", responded Uncle Bob.

Almost immediately Grandfather exploded, "They're not alike! They are no more alike than Heaven and Hell's alike!" The rest of the family had a very difficult time trying to suppress their open laughter. With a twinkle in his eye Uncle Bob went upstairs again and promptly returned with two blue socks.

Perhaps some would think of Uncle Bob as sometimes being the Devil's imp, but we should take note of the fact that he was combatting illness most of his life. It is logical to assume that Uncle Bob often teased someone a bit so that he and others could laugh. The newspaper account of his death stated, "— by his considerate and courteous treatment of all he made many friends who deeply sympathize with the bereaved family".

Proverbs 15: 15 (RSV) states: "All the days of the afflicted are evil, but a cheerful heart has a continual feast".

Chapter Twenty-Two
His First Car

The oldest of my Dad's generation was Uncle Simon. He always worked very hard, and because he helped to provide for his many brothers and sisters, he was married somewhat late in life. He ended up with seven of his own, though, and after they were all born be finally decided to purchase his first car. This would date him as being of late middle age when he decided to rely on a mechanical means of transportation.

Possibly because he had to serve as a sort of foster parent to some of his brothers and sisters, he was a strict disciplinarian with them. Similarly, he expected almost instant obedience from the horses he drove, according to my Dad and Uncle Ed who were recognized as good horsemen. They stated that even Uncle Simon knew that he was not a really good horseman. Like most farmers who had to use their hands to operate their farm implements as they drove, Uncle Simon usually directed his team by word of mouth rather than using the lines of the harness.

There came a time, though, when it seemed advisable for his family to own an automobile. Of course, all of Uncle Simon's children had been pressuring him to "get out of the middle ages", as they put it, and he could easily see that others were using their cars to travel farther away from their homes. Finally he said, "All right. We'll buy a car".

The first car he chose was a Star, probably a 1928 model. Of a blue color, it was known as a touring car, the popular body style of those days. Since at least three of his children were in their teens, and two of them had cars of their own, he chose one of them to drive the car home. For some time the family relied on one of the boys to drive when the family wanted to use their new car.

During this time Uncle Simon had been watching all the manipulations involved in operating his new motor vehicle. In opposition to his sense of pride, he frequently asked for driving details from any one of the boys who already knew how to drive. We may suspect that some of their answers puzzled him; the sudden transformation from being a horseman to a motorist would be a problem for nearly anyone.

One late spring Sunday afternoon Uncle Simon decided that he would take his turn at driving the car that was the family's pride. It was a beautiful day, which suited his plan perfectly. The boys who had cars were out driving, or were on dates, or had gone to a baseball game at the nearby town. You see, he was too proud to ask one of his sons to accompany him. Hadn't he closely observed everything they did when they drove? Besides, he didn't want anyone to be shouting advice and directions to him; that would probably interrupt his concentration. He recognized that he would certainly need all his powers of concentration when driving.

From here on, I'll let Uncle Simon tell his story the way he told it to me. "Well, I was proud of that car; I still am. Carrie (his wife) was settin' on the front porch. I told her what I was going to do and asked her if she wanted to take a ride with me. 'You go on ahead', she said, 'I'm enjoying this peace and quiet'.

"Well, I took the keys and got in the car. I started her up and touched all the gadgets as if I was driving; maybe I was gettin' up a little more courage, I don't know, but while I was settin' there I was also figurin' how to get out onto the road. Old Lizzie was in the drive right beside the house, so I figured that I could make a sharp turn on the lawn and be headed out to the road. You see, I didn't want to trust myself to backin' Lizzie up the very first thing. I was real careful, so I shifted gears and made the turn.

'That's not bad', I thought.

"I decided to go around the block, and when I got more out in the open, I would stop and start a few times, then learn how to back up. 'I did pretty well out there', I thought; 'I turned all the corners just like all the boys did, and I'm proud of how I backed up,' so I headed for home. 'Maybe Carrie will change her mind and go for a spin with me after she sees how I can manage this thing', I said to myself.

"Carrie was still settin' on the porch as I headed in the drive; I glanced at her, and right there my concentration was broke. I was headed right for the barnyard gate which was right beside the shed where we kept old Lizzie. I pulled back on the steering wheel and yelled, 'Whoa!' I pulled back all the harder, and I about pushed my feet through the floorboard. By the time I yelled 'Whoa!' again I went right through the gate. I tore it to smithereens!

"Carrie saw what was going on and she ran down the steps and yelled, 'Stop her!' I couldn't think of anything else to do so I drove right around the barn, through two more fences, and through the mud puddle next to the manure pile. My feet was so frozen to the floor I couldn't do a thing but steer; I guess I clean forgot where the brakes was.

"'Well', I decided, 'I'd better head out to the road to find out how to control this thing'. By that time the rest of the kids had come out and they was all shoutin', yellin' at me to do this and to do that. They was all yellin' at the same time, so I couldn't make out what they were sayin', but I was so busy steerin' that I couldn't listen, anyhow.

"I did try to hear what they said, so I turned my head toward them, and when I looked ahead, I was headed straight for Mom's flower bed. 'Stay away from my flowers!' she yelled at me.

"To heck with the flowers. Just get out of the way!" I yelled back, and right through the flowers I went. By then, there wasn't enough room to turn back into the drive, so around the house I went, tearin' out a couple of rose bushes that was ready to bloom. I did get out to the road when Fred drove up and saw what was the matter; he drove on down to the neighbors and waited for me there. By that time I was beginnin' to get hold of myself. I was rememberin' how to stop her when Fred jumped on the runnin' board and turned off the switch. Well, I don't need to tell you that he drove old Lizzie back home, and from that time on, I never forgot where the switch and the brakes was."

Every time I think of Uncle Simon's experience I smile to myself. Each of us can recall many episodes which spring out from the past to confront us. Perhaps there is a meaning or a lesson from each experience. It is obvious that Uncle Simon was not as prepared to drive a car as he had assumed; more than that, he let his overconfidence take precedence over sound judgement. An obvious moral to this experience can be found in Prov. 16: 18. A teaching of Jesus about preparedness and counting costs seems to be even more pertinent; we should consider the parable of the tower and the king going to war (Luke 14: 25-33). Out of verse 28, per RSV, comes the classic quotation: "For which of you, desiring to build a tower, does not first sit down and count the cost, whether he has enough to complete it?"

Chapter Twenty-Three
Throwing Stones

The Sunday gatherings at the Jairus Noecker home have been described elsewhere in this book, but the various activities in which the families were engaged has yet to be covered. The hustle and bustle of the women as they prepared and assembled the food for those large dinners should properly be left to our imaginations. The older children who were married would have brought prepared food with them to add to the meal. Of course, table settings and similar arrangements would have required less consideration than their concerns for the supply of a sufficient amount of food to satisfy the hungry assembly.

Characteristically, the men and boys would have been less feverishly occupied. Their principal activity would have been conversation. It is my understanding that Grandfather's philosophy and political views would be expressed with an appropriate amount of elocutionary skill. He was an accomplished orator, and he was obviously trained to present his views in a consistently logical manner. Because of this his opinions were seriously considered by the neighborhood, and certainly by his family.

After dinner the women would enjoy their own conversations which would involve methods of housekeeping, reports on the well-beings and accomplishments of each family member, plus some inevitable gossip. The men, conversely, frequently became involved in displaying various feats of strength which would include games, plus other demonstrations of skill.

According to one family member, an incident happened at the homestead one Sunday afternoon, which, as he related it, always caused him to break out into laughter as he recalled it. There were several years around the 1890's that many men and boys in the area had become interested in using slings of ancient design for throwing stones. These slings were very similar to the one that David used to kill Goliath. Simply, such a sling consists of an open pouch or pocket of leather. On either end or side of the pouch was fastened a string, or thong, preferably of rawhide. These strings were about 18 inches long, and the free end of one may have had a loop. To use the sling the loop would be slid on the thumb or middle finger of the thrower's hand. A round stone about the size of a hen's egg would be placed in the pouch. (Such stones were very plentiful in that part of Michigan). The other string's free end would be pulled up and grasped between thumb and forefinger of that same hand to keep the stone suspended by the sling. To throw the stone, the thrower would swing his throwing arm and sling around or over his head to extend his throwing arm's length. At the right instant during the forward swing the thrower would release the free end by releasing the grip of his thumb. The resultant increase in velocity would cause the stone to traverse a surprisingly great distance.

My Uncle Simon, the oldest of Jairus' children, was a very strong man; he was quite proficient in the use of such a sling, and the accuracy he achieved with it won the admiration of many. On this particular afternoon the men took up a contest of using a sling to determine who could throw the farthest distance. Uncle Simon's strength was beginning to show; he was outdistancing all the others. They were throwing from a spot in the pasture near Grandpa's barn toward a small marsh from which grew a few tall tamarack trees. The marsh was perhaps more than 150 yards away from the barn, but Uncle Simon's stones were reaching the trees. There were few of his competitors whose stones had reached that far.

A black youth who attended the school where the young Noeckers went happened to pass by on the road that led to the nearby town; he stopped to witness the contest. When Uncle Simon threw again, his stone knocked a few small limbs from the tamaracks. "Drop in dis fiel'," ("dropped in this field"), exclaimed the newcomer.

"Why, it did no such thing!" retorted Uncle Simon. "Now watch this!" With a mighty heave he released another stone; it landed farther in the grove.

With a sly wink at the others the boy assumed an air of authority and announced, "Dropped in dis fiel'", again.

Uncle Simon became exasperated to the amusement of all the others. Somewhat out of patience he accused the self-appointed umpire of the event of not noting distances correctly. "Now you look closely!" he shouted, and again he swung the sling with all his might. The third stone landed very near to where the second had gone. "See?", he demanded.

"Still drop in de fiel'", answered the impish youngster. By this time the rest of the men and boys were nearly doubled over with laughter. Uncle Simon seriously confronted the others because of their poorly concealed mirth; somehow he failed to see that they had become amused because he had been "taken in", as many described responses similar to his. He had mistakenly assumed that they were smiling because he couldn't throw farther than he had.

Soon the young black went on his way, and the contest ended; Uncle Simon continued to point out to the family that he really was throwing his stones into the grove, farther than the others could throw. "That boy just couldn't see good", he repeatedly explained.

Probably it was Solomon who wrote: "Only by pride cometh contention" (Proverbs 13: 10a [KJV]).

Chapter Twenty-Four
The Sleep-Walker

Uncle Henry Augustus Noecker was the eleventh child of my paternal grandparents; he was just older than my father. "Gust", as the family called him, was a sleep-walker. He died in middle age of what was then called "Bright's Disease". From the piecemeal information which I have been able to collect, he probably had some form of epilepsy. Possibly his frail health contributed to this odd behavior. Sometimes his nocturnal wanderings awoke other members of his family; they would get up, and lead him to his bed. Not even rousing from his sleep, he would not sleep-walk again that night.

During the 1890's Grandfather moved his family to a house that stood near the old Chapel Hill schoolhouse in Cass County, Michigan. The house was of the design which some called a "shotgun house'. By this, people meant that if both windows of the upstairs hall were open, a person could fire a shotgun in the one window, and the shot would go out the other without striking any part of the house. There were four bedrooms upstairs, with the kitchen, dining room, parlor, and a bedroom being downstairs. The family had not lived there long before summer arrived. One quiet sultry night they were awakened by a piercing scream, almost as if one were in terror. Rousing up they looked around and found Uncle Gust outside the house in a wheelbarrow. He had walked out through the upstairs hall window and had fallen into the wheelbarrow that was setting below. After checking him over for injuries and finding none, Grandpa and Grandma put Uncle Gust back in bed where he remained the rest of the night.

Before I continue with another anecdote about this uncle I must digress. Elsewhere, I have told of Grandfather's becoming a peddler. During his conversations with other peddlers he learned that hotels in larger cities were prospering due to the many traveling salesmen who were patrons. Instructing the boys of the family to gather all the nuts they could find each autumn, he announced that he was going to sell "goodies" to the hotel chefs. The entire family became involved in his project. On winter nights, immediately after supper, he and the boys would sit again around the kitchen table. He cracked the nuts carefully, and the boys would just as carefully pick out the nut kernels. They classified the nut-meats, because he sold the half-kernels for premium prices to confectioners and candy-makers who used these prized morsels to decorate the tops of their products. The fragments of the kernels were sold at lesser prices for use in cake batters and candy mixes. The women in the family did the packaging.

Understandably, the family income was meager. With all members of the family, the practice of thrift was not a matter of choice; it was a necessity. Each boy had a standing instruction from my Grandmother that before retiring at bedtime, he was to collect the nut-shells obtained from his nut-picking, and then deposit them on a newspaper which she had already laid on the floor near the cookstove. The reason for all this frugality was that nut-shells contain a surprising amount of oil. In the morning, when Grandmother wanted to start a fire in the cookstove, she wadded some paper, put it in the firebox, then laid the newspaper and nut-shells on the crumpled paper. Very soon after igniting the paper the shells would burst into a hot flame, and the stove would quickly be ready for cooking.

Before they went upstairs to bed to enjoy the bliss of sleep which only tired boys can know, they had a practice of leaving their high-top shoes near the stove. This usually provided for the luxury of prewarmed footwear when they arose and left bedrooms which often had sub-freezing temperatures. One year in particular, the boys were confronted by a perplexing and confusing mystery. As they came downstairs to put on their shoes, they were dismayed to find that their shoes were full of cracked nut-shells. This confronted them with an aggravating problem, because those shell fragments were sharp. More than that, they were difficult to dislodge entirely from certain recesses of their shoes. Each one noisily accused the other of doing such a mean trick. Just as noisy was the response from each one that he wouldn't even think of doing such a thing. The mystery wore on for perhaps longer than a month. Finally one of the older boys decided to "see for himself", as he put it. He pretended to go to bed with the others, but as soon as they were asleep he arose, and, fully clothed, he hid in the pantry nearby. It was the family custom to keep a dimly-lighted kerosene lamp in the kitchen to serve as an aid should an emergency occur.

The hours passed slowly by; the watchman nodded off to a doze several times, partially succumbing to the compelling desires of a youthful, growing, tired body. He roused himself again, and soon he heard the kitchen clock strike the hour of one. Suddenly there was a very slight rustling sound, then he heard soft footsteps. He hid as carefully behind the door as the crowded pantry would permit, and into the shadowy semi-darkness the figure of a boy appeared. It was Gust! Very methodically Gust shuffled to the pile of nut-shells. Picking up the newspaper which held them, he systematically used the paper as a chute to fill each shoe. Leaving the residue on the sheet he returned the paper and its contents to its original location, and with a bear-like shuffle he slowly climbed the stairs and returned to his bed.

The next morning when Gust was confronted with his nocturnal prank he hotly denied it. He even firmly maintained that he had never left his bed until morning. After repeated accusations and subsequent denials the issue was dropped, because the hour of another hard day's work had arrived. Somehow, the event was scarcely mentioned again that day; the entire family recalled Gust's other sleep-walking episodes. Later in the week another brother secretly made a pact with two others that he would be the watchman that night. The watch was fruitless, due to the fact that Gust did his sleep-walking only after he had become unduly fatigued.

Night watches were repeated at irregular intervals, and finally Gust appeared again to repeat his nocturnal behavior. This time the brother grabbed Gust and called to the family for help. Gust instinctively struggled to free himself, then awakened. By this time most of the family had presented themselves in the kitchen to find out the cause of the disturbance. Of course Gust was peppered with a host of questions regarding the meaning and cause of his actions. Sheepishly, he had little to say in his defense. Embarrassed and confused, he returned to bed as soon as he could. For some unexplainable reason, Gust never again repeated his innocent prank. Family peace was restored.

While Gust's prank could not be assessed as being evil, the whole series of events should remind us of our responsibilities to each other. James wrote: "My brethren, if any one among you wanders from the truth and someone brings him back, let him know that whoever brings back a sinner from the error of his way will save his soul from death and will cover a multitude of sins" (James 5: 19, 20).

Chapter Twenty-Five
Sunday Schools

Public schools and the old one-room schoolhouses have contributed a far greater influence on the moral and religious life in this country than most people realize. As the pioneers pushed westward to establish themselves in what had been a wilderness, they set up elementary schools for their children soon after they had constructed living quarters for themselves. These schools soon required buildings with facilities for teaching the essentials of education.

History and legend bring to us an abundance of accounts of hasty and lawless actions which occurred along the frontier. Although the settlers in a new community may not have had a common religious background, they recognized their need for a stable religious influence as a true basis for all morality. Naturally, they turned to setting up non-sectarian Sunday Schools which met in the schoolhouses. Teaching responsibilities in the Sunday Schools fell largely to women, although there were devout men who also contributed much toward religious education.

When Grandfather moved his family to Cass County in Michigan, he settled near Baldwin Lake in Porter Township, in the southeast corner of the county. His children attended the Chapel Hill grammar school nearby. By the time my father attended, Mr. Daniel Eby was the teacher. He was a good Christian man, and possibly due to his efforts a Sunday School was established, meeting in the schoolhouse. Whenever the opportunity presented itself, a worship service which included a sermon followed the session of learning.

Elsewhere it has been suggested that Grandfather must have become thoroughly disenchanted and discouraged from continuing in the pastoral ministry, for by this time (the late 1890's) he rarely attended worship services. When these sessions began at Chapel Hill, he insisted that his children should be regular attenders. On one particular Sunday morning, as Dad and Uncle George returned home, they announced that there had been preaching that day.

"There was? Who preached? What did he talk about?" asked Grandfather.

"I don't know who he was," Uncle George replied, "But he kept saying 'Amack-ah-rye! Amack-ah-rye!'"

"Oh, no!" exclaimed Grandfather.

"Oh, yes!" Uncle George responded, "How do you know what he said? You weren't there!"

Grandfather shouted back, "I didn't have to be there! I know what he was saying. He was talking about the Prodigal Son, and when the son started to go back home to his father, his father saw him 'makran'." (He pronounced it "mack-ran"). Grandfather concluded, "That's the Greek word meaning 'afar off!' " Grandfather then completed the meaning of the parable about the lost son in a manner that Dad never forgot.

Uncle George, on the other hand, seemed to remember the incident with some bitterness. I knew Uncle George rather well, and as far as I know, he never made his commitment to the Lord, and he rarely attended a worship service. Paul instructed the Christians at Ephesus, "Fathers, do not provoke your children to anger, but bring them up in the discipline and instruction of the Lord" (Eph. 6: 4, RSV).

Chapter Twenty-Six
A Tug of War

As they should be, most family reunions are joyous occasions. Because so many people are gathered there, those who have attended frequently discover that after most families have departed for their homes there has only been time to do little more than exchanging greetings to some. My family has agreed that almost invariably, those who we saw the least were the ones with whom we really had wanted to talk and share experiences. Then, too, there were those family potluck dinners with too much to eat and too little time to enjoy it before other events were demanding our attentions elsewhere. From out of the maze of contacts we did manage to make - the information we learned about the others, and the wonderful fellowship we enjoyed - these events usually stand out quite clearly in our memories.

The Noecker reunions were almost always held at a picnic area beside one of the many lakes in southern Michigan. Dad, Mother and I lived in Illinois, and a trip to Michigan required a long day's journey (by T-model Ford limitations), so we did not attend these events regularly. Probably because of that, there are several reunions which live on quite vividly in my memory. Perhaps because I was small at that time, perhaps because Uncle Simon was the oldest and largest in stature of all my aunts and uncles, my attentions were usually focused on him and his activities. I was quite impressed by the shock of wavy white hair which crowned his head.

In order to give a better picture of Uncle Simon, it should be stated that, being the oldest in the family, it was natural for him to assume the role and responsibilities of being a surrogate parent. Perhaps, because he was the tallest, he became recognized as fitted for this important niche in the family set-up. Being a very strong man, he had the endurance of a mule, and he was proud of his remarkable dexterity and ability in doing all sorts of farm work. His neighbors sometimes acknowledged his abilities as a woodsman by stating in exaggeration, "That man could lay a tree limb on a stone, then take an axe and cut it in two without nicking the axe on the stone!"

During this particular reunion, after the enormous picnic dinner which was a tradition with the family, the men turned to their usual contests of physical skill and strength. A foot race was planned, the object being to run to a marked line on the sod and return to the starting line - a total length of probably less than 200 yards. A number of younger members of the family gathered at the starting line, so Uncle Simon also entered. The result of the race was that three or more young men beat Uncle Simon to the finish, so he promptly got all of the family together and challenged anyone to another race with him. The length suggested was ten miles! Of course, he got no takers.

A few years later, when I was about nine years old, we again attended the scheduled reunion. As usual, after dinner and the conducting of some routine business which included reading correspondence from those not able to attend that year, the men turned to their athletic events. My Uncle Harvey had brought along a hay-rope. This was a one-inch manila rope which was used to hoist large clutches of hay from a hay-rack up to the hay-mow in a barn. He suggested that we choose up sides and have a Tug of War contest. The tug was a hard-fought one, and at its conclusion someone proposed that the men of Dad's generation should pull against an equal number of men from the younger second generation. That was agreed upon and the new Tug of War began. As I recall it, the older men won.

Except at funerals, friendly banterings, sometimes arguments, almost always occurred during Noecker gatherings. This reunion was no exception. Uncle Harvey, one of my older uncles, liked to contribute his share of teasing, starting family "discussions". Once in a while, an innocent prank could be attributed to him. This time, while the men had gone back to the table for lemonade or coffee to refresh themselves before the traditional baseball game, Uncle Harvey asked Max and Drexel, two of my cousins about my age and myself to come with him to where the Tug of War contests had been staged. His proposal remains clearly in my memory: "I want you boys to take on Simon in a Tug of War." (He didn't say "your Uncle Simon", because my older cousin, Max, was Simon's youngest son). He continued, "I know you can do it; you boys are good and strong. All you need to do is just take your stand and pull hard. Simon will accept the challenge; I know how to get him fired up. He'll be eager to show that he was the main contributor in the other pulls. When the pull gets started Simon will get himself set and try to pull you boys along by brute strength. Just hold your ground for a minute, then start pulling harder as you back up. Once you get him started, keep pulling till you get him across the line! Once he has to give ground, don't give him a chance to get set again! You can do it. Is that OK with you?"

We nodded in agreement, so the fun began. We were lined up with Max in the lead; I was in the middle, and Drexel, the youngest and the heaviest, on the end. We all grasped the rope, took our stances, then someone shouted, "Go!"

Right away it became obvious that we were novices in this kind of sport. Uncle Simon started to pull us forward a foot or so, then Uncle Harvey shouted, "Come on! You're not pulling! You can do it!" We were still in a sort of crouch when Drexel started to use his weight to squat. We could see that this caused Uncle Simon to be dislodged slightly from his position, so I squatted, then Max followed. That accomplished the job! Uncle Simon tried vainly to "get set" again, but we never let him have the chance to do so. We pulled him, feet first, across the line. When he stood up we could see that his shoes no longer had heels; he had literally pulled them off his shoes!

We felt really proud that we had been able to out-do Uncle Simon, but many years later I realized that Uncle Simon had been "snookered" into an almost impossible match. Although he was over six feet tall, he couldn't have weighed more than 190 pounds. Our combined weight was probably more than 350 pounds, and Uncle Simon was "a born loser", as we would term it today. Poor Uncle Simon had to endure the jokes his brothers made about his getting so old that he couldn't out-pull three nine-year-olds. All that afternoon Uncle Simon went around showing everyone that his heels had come off, and that if they would have stuck on he would have "pulled those kids all over the place."

Truly, all of Uncle Simon's brothers, my Dad included, readily admitted that he was the strongest one in the family. After some years of this honest praise, Uncle Simon had become over-confident of his strength.
Solomon observed: "The glory of young men is their strength, but the beauty of old men is their gray hair" (Proverbs 20: 29).

Chapter Twenty-Seven
Concerned or Carefree

My uncle Harvey was a good farmer, but he tended to fret a lot; his nervous condition was somewhat contagious, because his attitude and comments often tempted those associated with him to be similarly affected. Aunt Maude, Harvey's wife, was not at all inclined to share her husband's fretfulness. When she spoke, her statements usually included a bit of philosophy which was partially disguised with a touch of humor. Uncle would often remark that the weather did not suit the needs of the farmers who were working so hard to "make ends meet". Quite often she responded that if we could control the conditions about us, we probably would institute such frequent radical changes that the whole order of the universe would become upset. Then, with an affectionate smile and a slight nod of her head, she would conclude her remarks somewhat like this, "Do you think, Harvey dear, that you would really want to have control over all these conditions about which you are complaining?"

Aunt Maude had a brother, Henry Bedell, who was a bachelor. Being a day-laborer (farmers called them "farm hands"), he often stayed with Harvey and Maude during the winter months, doing whatever odd jobs there were to do around the farm. Henry tried to be like his sister, so quite often he displayed a "devil may care" attitude.

One year, well into the winter, my Dad also came to stay at Uncle Harvey's for a couple of weeks. Both Dad and Henry enjoyed going out into the timber to cut firewood for their hosts, so they immediately developed a strong liking for each other. Harvey appreciated this help, because their provision of fuel allowed him to do some odd jobs around the barn; many of these jobs had been set aside for months due to the lack of available time.

Being a realist, as soon as he had completed his "pick-up work", he seized this opportunity to build up a big wood-pile which would last on into the summer months. He remarked, "Well, since you fellows are willing to help with the wood cutting, I'll go to the timber with you for a few days. In that way we can have our wood-cutting out of the way by the time spring comes."

At the woods the next day, it was decided that Henry and Dad should use Harvey's two-man cross-cut saw to cut the logs into stove-length blocks, and Uncle Harvey would split the cut blocks into sticks that would fit the cook stove and heating stoves. Harvey surveyed the waiting logs, then made a mark on one of them with his axe. "You cut to here, and that's enough for today", he stated. Henry winked at Dad, and they stripped off their jackets and shirts; they sawed as if in desperation. Just before noon they had more than finished their day's allotment.

Not waiting for Harvey, they hurried to the house. Henry sat down at Aunt Maude's parlor organ, and Dad, taking his cue from Henry, picked up the violin he had been trying to learn to play. Neither one knew how to play even a simple tune, but when they saw Harvey approaching, each one played his instrument, employing the actions of professionals. The din was terrific. Aunt Maude was openly laughing as she finished preparations for dinner - she never hurried. Uncle Harvey was irritated and frustrated by the cacophony; after washing he sat at the kitchen table, drumming his fingers as if to say, "Maude, please hurry!"

After dinner Uncle Harvey donned his outer wear, then looking toward the other two, he said, "Come on, boys, let's go to work!"
"Oh no," responded Henry, "You told us to cut to your mark. We cut two blocks past that. We're done for the day". So saying, he leaned back in Harvey's favorite rocking chair. Harvey protested, then recognized defeat;

he turned and headed for the woods. Aunt Maude exploded in mirth.

At another day in the woods, as they finished their lunch, Henry stepped up on a stump. Looking about and waving his arms, he asked, "Harvey, I don't suppose you ever saw me doing a back-somersault from a stump, did you?"

Harvey's response was, "No, I never did".

"I guess you never will!" ended that conversation.

Henry was not able to entirely withstand the contagion of his brother-in-law's fretfulness, however. That winter in the mid 1890's had dragged on; it had been a long, severely cold season, causing the springtime to be noticeably later than usual. Henry, like most farmers in the area, became restless, anxious to begin farmwork so he could earn wages again. The nearby lakes were still frozen solid. Turning to Uncle Harvey who was standing nearby, he shook his head and asked, "How is it ever going to warm up with all the ice in the lakes?" After a pause of a few moments, he innocently asked again, "And how in the world is the ice going to get out of the lakes until it does warm up?"

Henry did not mind working on places high above-ground; Uncle Harvey did. Consequently, when the windmill needed to be lubricated or repaired Henry was always asked to do the job. Early one morning, since he knew that the windmill would be needing attention, he quietly climbed up the derrick to reach the machinery. It wasn't long before Uncle Harvey couldn't see him. "Where's Henry?" he asked my Dad.

Before Dad could answer, Henry stood up on the little platform beside the fan of the windmill, and with gestures imitating an orator, he sonorously spoke, "Sex, seffulous, syramus! The rest of us, Bam-Bam us!"

"Henry! Come down from there, before you break your fool neck", exclaimed Uncle Harvey. With his work done, Henry climbed down to the earth.

Not long afterward, the trustees of the town of Constantine approached Henry to see if he would undertake the job of painting the town's water tower. Henry agreed to take the job, but one night, before the paint arrived for the project, Henry had a vivid dream. He told my Dad that in the dream he was painting the water tower when he fell off. He immediately decided to cancel his agreement with them.

In to-day's stressful times we especially need to heed the wisdom of Jesus: "Therefore I tell you, do not be anxious about your life, what you shall eat or what you shall drink, nor about your body, what you shall put on. Is not life more than food, and the body more than clothing? Look at the birds of the air: they neither sow nor reap nor gather into barns, and yet your heavenly Father feeds them. Are you not of much more value than they? And which of you by being anxious can add one cubit to his span of life? And why are you anxious about clothing? Consider the lilies of the field, how they grow; they neither toil nor spin; yet I tell you, even Solomon in all his glory was not arrayed like one of these. But if God so clothes the grass of the field, which today is alive and tomorrow in thrown into the oven, will He not much more clothe you, O men of little faith? Therefore do not be anxious, saying, 'What shall we eat?' or 'What shall we drink?' or 'What shall we wear?' For the Gentiles seek all these things; and your heavenly Father knows that you need them all. But seek first His kingdom and His righteousness, and all these things shall be yours as well.

"Therefore do not be anxious about tomorrow, for tomorrow will be anxious for itself. Let the day's own trouble be sufficient for the day." (Matthew 6: 25-34, RSV).

Chapter Twenty-Eight
Adopted Calves

During the mid 1970's my cousin, Max, sent me a scarcely distinguishable picture which follows this story. It shows a cow and calf in front of the wide, low-spreading barn which was Grandfather's. He is standing behind the cow with his right hand resting on her back. The left side of the picture, shows two men leaning on a fence, facing the cow and calf. The one on the extreme left is Dave Arbogast who is smiling broadly. Next to him is a neighbor, Harold "Hod" Reif, who sold the animals to Grandfather; he is also smiling. In the doorway of the barn stands a girl of probably eight or nine, and above, looking out from the rather low hayloft door, is a mischievous-appearing boy. (His story will have to wait until later).

Quoting from the letter which Max wrote to accompany the picture, there is this account: "—— the guy in the middle of the picture sold Granddad a cow with calf. When he got them home, the cow kicked the bejabbers out of the calf when it tried to feed. So Granddad took the cow back and demanded his money back because the calf didn't belong to the cow. The other guy then said that he knew the calf belonged to the cow because he gave the calf to her."

The story of the adoption of that calf spread all over the vicinity, so the editor of the Constantine, Michigan newspaper decided that the local flavor of this story would make it news-worthy. He arranged for a photographer to go with him to Grandfather's farm. There they got the seller and his neighbor to pose with Grandfather as he stood beside the animals. The story and accompanying picture was published in the newspaper, and soon the account was humorously talked about all over southern Michigan. I still chuckle about the event whenever I think of it.

Having had similar problems with orphaned young animals when I was growing up on the farm, I recall the general unwillingness of cows to become foster mothers to strange calves. We had a red Milking Shorthorn cow, one item of the livestock which Dad took over from a farmer who had defaulted in his mortgage payments; we called her "Old Red". Far from looking like a "Shorthorn", Old Red had horns which would have made almost any Texas longhorn cow proud to own. Poor Old Red! She was something of a rebel; because of her prodigious horns she bossed all the other cows. Before we ever tried to milk her, we could see by the looks of her udder that she produced a lot of milk. We did all our milking by hand, so we could foresee trouble. The teats on her udder were so small that milking her would be a real task. We estimated that milking her would take about twice the time required to milk any other cow. At last, in desperation, Dad announced, "The next time that Old Red has a calf, she's going to keep it. I'll not milk her any more after she goes dry!" Neither Mother or I protested his decision.

The next spring Old Red had her new calf - a dandy red heifer. During that same week, Old Snow, our white cow had a white heifer calf, too. Scratching his head, Dad thought aloud, "With all the milk that Old Red gives, I wonder if she could suckle two calves." That evening he put Old Red in a separate stall and turned both the red and white calves in with her. What a fight Old Red put up! She tried to shelter her own while butting and kicking the white one whenever she got near to suckle. It was immediately obvious that Old Red would never accept the white one, even when it was shut in alone with her.

Finally, Dad decided to solve the problem by putting an anti-kick chain on Old Red whenever he wanted both calves to feed. This device consisted of a rather light weight chain about fifteen inches long; on each end was a flat hook. When the chain was put on a cow, the first hook grasped the large tendon just above the knee of one hind leg. When the chain was passed around the front of each leg, the other hook grasped the other large tendon. Thus tethered, a cow could neither kick nor take a step; she was forced to remain in that location.

When evening came again, Dad put the chain on Old Red, then let the calves in to her. Red nearly fell down, trying to kick or walk away; her hind legs could be of no use to her, so she tried to fight the white calf away by throwing her horned head around to butt it. Both calves were hungry, and they pressed close to her side to avoid her attempts to thrash about. Red was defeated, and she knew it. Somewhere in my files there is a snapshot I took of her and the calves at feeding time. The calves are getting their nourishment while Old Red's horny head is thrown back, as if to appeal to a higher authority, asking, "Why do I have to put up with this? Is there no justice?"

The situation surrounding that white calf often comes back in my recollections of days back on the farm. That calf was eager to be adopted; she was hungry!

To the Galatians Paul wrote: "But when the time had fully come, God sent forth His Son, born of woman, born under the law, to redeem those who were under the law, so that we might receive adoption as sons. And because you are sons, God has sent His Spirit into our hearts, crying, 'Abba! Father!' So through God you are no longer a slave but a son, and if a son then an heir" (Gal. 4: 4-7 RSV). What an inheritance!

When the story about the adopted calf became known throughout the community, the local newspaper (name unknown) had the men who were involved in the incident to pose in front of Grandfather's barn, with the cow and calf, for a picture. The picture, accompanied by an article describing the incident appeared in the next issue of the paper. Left to right: Dave Arbogast, Harold "Hod" Reif, Jairus Noecker. The children in the picture are unknown.

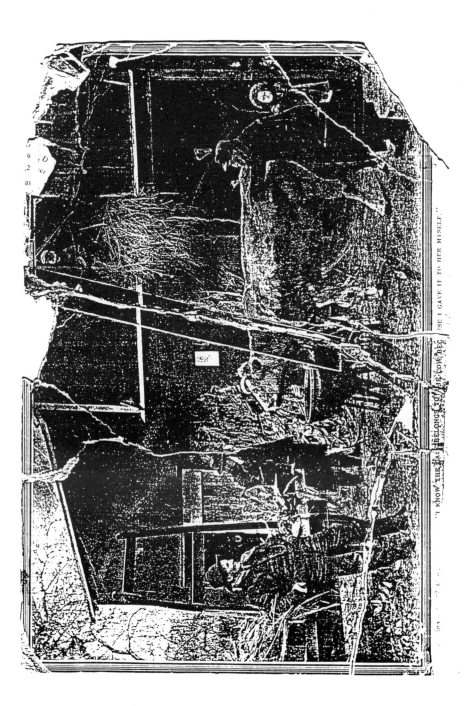

"I KNOW THE CAT BELONGS TO THE CONSTABLE, BECAUSE I GAVE IT TO HER MYSELF."

Additional Family History